Spécialités de la Maison

The American Friends of France

Foreword by Graydon Carter

Preface by Christine Schwartz Hartley

COLLINS DESIGN
An Imprint of HarperCollinsPublishers

First published in 2010 by
Collins Design
An Imprint of HarperCollins*Publishers*
10 East 53rd Street
New York, NY 10022
Tel: (212) 207-7000
Fax: (212) 207-7654
collinsdesign@harpercollins.com
www.harpercollins.com

Distributed throughout the world by
HarperCollins*Publishers*
10 East 53rd Street
New York, NY 10022
Fax: (212) 207-7654

Library of Congress control number:
2009933558

Design by Erica Deahl

Printed in USA
Second Printing, 2010

Publisher's Note
Spécialités de la Maison was originally published in 1940. The recipes and cooking instructions have been re-created here exactly as they appeared in the original book. HarperCollins*Publishers* has neither tested these recipes nor guarantees that they are fully compatible with contemporary cooking methods.

Contents

Foreword

———

In the summer of 1940—as great swaths of France fell under the authority of Germany's Vichy government—the possibility of a future without the franc or bouillabaisse seemed chillingly real. And while history tells us that life has gone on without the former, it's almost impossible to imagine it without the latter.

The appearance, around the same time, of a slim, delightful volume called *Spécialités de la Maison* now seems refreshingly anachronistic, as does the name of the group that published it: the American Friends of France—a charity founded by J. P. Morgan's daughter Anne. The case, wrapped in red-and-white checked cloth, evoked a romantic, candlelit dinner for two. The book jacket was designed by Clement Hurd, who would go on to illustrate the Margaret Wise Brown books, including the eternally magical *Goodnight Moon*. The preface was by Louis Bromfield, a decorated veteran of the Front during World War I, who returned from France, became a Pulitzer Prize-winning novelist, and then went on to become a pioneer of sustainable farming. So even before you got to the actual recipes—and there were some doozies—this volume already had an admirable pedigree. The charming dishes and their preparations included in the book—described by their prominent sponsors with a bygone era's fondness for language ("spread each side of sandwich with just a suspicion of mayonnaise")—beckoned a budding American international palate, which would take full flower after World War II.

In the seven decades between the original publication of
Spécialités and this timely and inspired re-issue, shepherded
by writer and translator Christine Schwartz Hartley, the culinary
landscape has changed in ways both large and small. When
this book debuted, France was the unquestioned center of the
gastronomical universe. These days you can find as sumptuous a
coq au vin on the streets of Chicago or New York as you can on the
broad boulevards of Haussmann's Paris. In the old days, remember,
dinner in many parts of this country could accurately be
described as an intermezzo between the cherished cocktail hour
and the beloved nightcap. Now that both of those adult pleasures
have fallen victim to workouts and 10:30 bedtimes, dinner has
become the main event.

While dining circa 1940 may have been an unspectacular
pastime for most Americans, this did not appear to be the case
with *Spécialités de la Maison*'s contributors, a starry cavalcade
of the best and brightest from all walks of public life. Recipes
from the world of show business include Katharine Hepburn's
"Chicken Burgundy Style," Clifton Webb's "Pommes de Terre
Frites," Mrs. Samuel Goldwyn's "Golden Gate Salad," and
Charlie Chaplin's "Sour Cream Hot Cakes," among others.
Morgan rounded up Pearl S. Buck ("Sweetsour Fish"), Aldous
Huxley ("Paella à la Valenciana"), and Condé Nast, who offered
his recipe for cooking Smithfield Ham. Herbert Bayard Swope
presented his regimen for preparing perfect hamburger patties,
a technique that is not unlike Martha Stewart's. ("They should
be firm, but not too closely packed.") Morgan got both Lunts,
with Alfred's "Russian Meat Loaf" and Lynn Fontanne's
"Broiled Duckling," as well as Noël Coward's "Filet of
Chevreuil," Katharine Cornell's "Frog Legs Sauté Salonaise,"
and Deems Taylor's recipe for "Quick Cheese Soufflé"—"Eat

very hot and very quickly, as it turns into morocco leather in about six minutes."

There are recipes from prominent restaurants of the day, including Jack and Charlie's "21" (still doing business as "21"), Voisin, and the Colony. And this being a book compiled by someone named Morgan, *Spécialités de la Maison* is liberally sprinkled with offerings from other moneyed American names: Cabot, Cushing, duPont, Rockefeller, Vanderbilt, Harriman, Pennoyer, Pell, and Astor. Morgan even includes one of her own, for "Champagne Punch."

Taken as a whole, dishes such as Norma Shearer's "Lentil Soup" ("serve the croutons fried in butter"), Laurence Olivier's "Moules Farcies" (with *two* glasses of dry white wine), and William Rhinelander Stewart's "Will's Famous Eggs" (served with toast fried in bacon grease) are a pleasant reminder of those blissfully guilt-free days of American adulthood before stationary bikes, energy bars, and the Atkins diet. Some of these illustrious people may have suspected that their world was teetering on the brink, and in a way it was. But, please, for the moment, allow Helen Keller to enjoy her "Lobster à la Newburg," the Duc de Verdura his "Tomato and Clams," Fanny Brice her "Yorkshire Hot Pot," and Mrs. Astor her "Steak Eros." Just remember, Shearer lived to be 81, Olivier 82, and Keller 88. Anita Loos's recipe for "Liverburger" went like this: "Drop [spoonfuls of ground liver and bread soaked in cream] into hot olive oil and fry. Serve with crisp bacon and hashed-in-cream potatoes." Yum. And Loos was around to celebrate her 93rd birthday. Do not tell me there isn't a lesson to be learned from all this.

Graydon Carter
October 2009, New York City

Preface

The minute I discovered *Spécialités de la Maison* among a rare-
and antique-book dealer friend's stock, I knew I had come across
what the French call *une vraie trouvaille*—a real find. A New
Yorker for the last two decades, I was born French and brought up
properly, so I don't usually boast or get carried away. But this
little cookbook swept me off my feet, and I am very proud and
happy to be bringing it back to life.

A compendium of more than two hundred recipes first collected
in 1940—and expanded in 1949—to raise funds for the now-
defunct war-relief organization, the American Friends of France,
Spécialités de la Maison is an improbable Who's Who of a glam-
orous international smart set as well as an indirect snapshot of
America's *entre-deux-guerres* hedonist elite. For here, as Graydon
Carter so elegantly notes, are some of the era's best writers, artists, and tastemakers, as well as eminent socialites and political
folk (the nation's First Lady, Eleanor Roosevelt, no less!), offering
recipes for dishes and drinks they enjoyed alone, *en famille*, or
with friends, and all for a good cause: to help the French popula-
tion face the wreckage of another world war. A thrillingly direct
and amusing link to this scintillating crowd's cuisine, *Spécialités'*
recipes also speak volumes about their authors' origins, person-
alities, or positions in society. Condensed biographies for a large
number of the contributors are featured at the end of the book,

and there are myriad personal and professional connections between them.

Above all, *Spécialités de la Maison* is a stunning encapsulation of Anne Morgan's life. As the youngest of financier J. Pierpont Morgan's four children, she was born in 1873 into America's moneyed aristocracy and soon developed a deep love for France through countless "seasons" spent there with her parents. Friendships with pioneering theatrical and literary agent-producer Elisabeth Marbury and ineffable actress-turned-interior decorator Elsie de Wolfe provided a powerful introduction to the world of entertainment and fun. By 1913, Morgan was part owner of the historic Villa Trianon in Versailles and, with these two women, hosted legendary parties for their cosmopolitan artist and society friends. By 1916, she was helping finance Marbury's first Broadway production of *See America First* by a young Cole Porter (see page 152), which featured Clifton Webb (see page 158), among other actors. Morgan's lifelong attachments—society, France, and the arts—were now set.

A horrifying visit to France's battlefields in 1914 led Morgan to dedicate herself to relieving its citizens' suffering, and in this work she proved herself to be incredibly willful, enterprising, hardworking, and committed. The extent of Morgan's efforts, which included but were not limited to raising and disbursing more than $5 million for medical aid, food, and reconstruction between 1918 and 1924, were twice recognized by the French government: with the Croix de Guerre in 1917, and again in 1932, with the Legion of Honor. Morgan thus became the order's first American woman Commander. Many years and multiple good works later, convinced that another war was inevitable, Morgan, by then in her sixties, founded American Friends of France, the fund-raising arm of her

Paris–based Comité Américain de Secours Civil, which was set-ting up relief centers for evacuees. In this extraordinary little book, Morgan mobilized her wide circle of friends to appeal to American citizens' support for what would be her last, and most intense, effort. She died in 1952, four years after ill health forced her to retire. She was unquestionably *une grande dame*.

Christine Schwartz Hartley
October 2009

Introduction

——

Good food is closely allied to civilization and the most civilized countries in the world are those which have the most comprehensive and complicated list of dishes. I think at once of France, China, India and Sweden—countries in which good food has always shared importance with music, literature, philosophy and all forms of art. I take it for granted that the purchaser of this book will be interested in the subject of food, a subject upon which miles of nonsense have been talked and written.

I say "nonsense" because everyone, however ignorant, is entitled to the privilege of speaking on food, and rightly, since one dish may be one man's food and another's poison. If a cowboy likes catsup on mashed potatoes, then to him, catsup on mashed potatoes is a delicious dish. I, myself, have never been able to see any virtue in *tripes à la mode de Caen*, but I am willing to concede that to others it may be a dish of supreme delicacy and importance. I, myself, happen to enjoy cottage cheese and maple syrup, a concoction which may well be regarded as barbaric, but which on examination proves merely to be another variation of the classic French dessert of cream cheese and Bar-le-Duc.

What I am driving at is the nonsense and impertinence of people who praise extravagantly what they think is smart to praise and condemn with proportionate violence anything either new or at variation with what they, in their snob's education, have been

taught to believe impossible. Snobbery in food is responsible for
most of the rot we are treated to. One of the silliest statements one
hears over and over again is that there is no good food to be had in
England. Usually it is uttered by people who have never been to
England or who have adventured in British food only as far as
Simpson's Restaurant. Another equally silly bromide is the one
about being able to find a wonderful meal wherever you stop in
France. Some of the best food I have ever eaten has been prepared
by English cooks in great London houses and country places and
some of the vilest I have ever eaten has been at wayside restaurants
in France. The French chef who excels at complicated sauces frequently fails at simpler dishes because as a rule he has no proper
respect for the essential flavor of the vegetable, meat or fish itself.
To the average French chef, the freshness and prime flavor of a vegetable is of small importance; he will remedy the loss of freshness
by seasoning. Whether peas are ten days old or picked fresh from
the garden with the dew on them is a matter of small importance.
In this, I firmly believe, he is absolutely wrong. God made the sin-
gular delicious flavor of new peas (which the English cook respects)
and not even a French chef has been able to improve on it.

And there is the school of snob who thinks earnestly that no
dish can be good unless it is complicated by seasonings and
sauces. I can think of nothing more monstrous or stomach-turn-
ing than an unrelieved diet based on the *haute cuisine*. I know, for
I once had a cook who made the most magnificent *plats* but could
not properly create a simple baked potato (incidentally one of the
greatest of delicacies). And there is the snob who believes that
anything not of French origin is absurd—the sort who speaks
contemptuously of such things as *Ladies' Home Journal* fruit
salad—an excellent dish whose only fault is that it should never

have been called a salad but an *entremet* and which has high points both on the score of delicacy and of health.

I am a great believer in regional food and believe that if you want the best food you should eat French food in France, American food in America, English food in England. I speak out of experience and with sound reasons, because local materials, their quality and their freshness, are the foundation of good food. Nobody in his right mind can believe that filet of American flounder Marguery has the same delicacy as filet of Channel sole prepared in the same way. There are no chickens in the world like the chickens of France. A *poulet de Bresse* has a special and unique flavor, tenderness, juiciness and delicacy because it is a special breed, because it is fed on French grass and herbs, because before it is killed it has been fed milk and garlic and parsley, and because it has been freshly killed—a combination which is not and perhaps cannot be produced elsewhere. A Gruyère cheese can only be produced in the canton of Vaud in Switzerland and American Gruyère, while delicious, is not real Gruyère. Sweet corn, one of the earth's great delicacies, is simply not sweet corn outside of the Mississippi basin. French asparagus has something, I do not know what—and I mean green asparagus, not the horrible woody white varieties—which asparagus in America lacks, no matter how you cook it nor how you dress it.

One thing which both the French and Chinese recognize and honor is the *texture* of food. I have alluded to it in my own salad recipe. One sort of salad should be crisp; another is at its best only when made of wilted lettuces. Cucumbers, under certain circumstances should be crisp, under others wilted. The Chinese-American dish of chicken chow-mein and almonds is a corruption of Chinese cooking occurring in America but its excellence is so great (when properly made) that the dish has found its way back to China and been accepted as a new Chinese dish. Its merit lies, I think, not only in the variety of flavors which reach the tongue, but also in the variety of textures of food which go to make up the dish—the hard and the soft foods mixed, with a difference even in the hardness and softness of each ingredient. It is a dish which provides sensation not only to the sense of taste but to that of feeling as well. There is the softness of the rice and the different softness of the fried onions, the crispness of the celery and the different crispness of the water chestnut, the hardness of the fried noodles and the different hardness of the almonds, and so on. Each mouthful is different, each one a surprise combination both of flavor and texture. One's tongue is never bored as with the sameness in flavor and texture of *pommes de terre vapeur*, to my mind, one of the inexcusably rapid and horrible, simple foods.

This note of introduction has been rambling and discursive, the mere statement of a few random thoughts upon a fascinating subject which merits volumes. An excellent French cook once said to me, "You will never have a good cook in a house where they do not care about food. No good cook could abase herself to work in such a household for any amount of money." That is a thought to cherish for its truth and for the profoundness of the thought behind it. A man indifferent to food not only is uncivilized, he is without a soul.

As for the purpose to which the sale of this excellent and interesting book is dedicated, there is no need for explanation or commendation. The proceeds of its sale will go to help those who are fighting for civilization and in civilization the art of cooking holds a high place. This book with its collection of new and excellent recipes collected from among those who respect and value good cooking, is worth its price many times over. The cause for which it is being sold is a great one. By buying it you will gain treasures both on earth and in heaven.

Louis Bromfield

Recipes

——

Appetizers

—

Cheese and Sardine Mousse

6 Philadelphia cream cheeses	2 cans sardines
½ cup parsley	Rind and juice of 1 lemon
1 bottle capers	½ cup mint (chopped fine)
Paprika	Hot toast
Salt	

Press into mold or ring and serve with thin hot toast.

Mrs. R. H. Carleton, New York City

Sandwich Filling

6 packages cream cheese	2 tsps. horseradish sauce
1 bunch watercress	

Chop watercress very fine, add to cream cheese. Blend well and add horseradish sauce.

Miss Anne Morgan, New York City

Mushroom Sandwiches

1 lb. mushrooms	Mayonnaise
Salt	Pepper

Hash very fine 1 lb. mushrooms (heads and tails) and put in large copper pan with a little fresh butter. Stir over medium fire from time to time for 5 minutes. Season very well with ground pepper and salt. Cover for 15 minutes over very low fire and the juice will come out. When done, drain off juice through sieve and put mushrooms in bowl and cool. Spread each side of sandwich with just a suspicion of mayonnaise so it will hold. Keep sandwiches in wax paper and leave 1 hour in ice box before serving.

Mrs. Douglas Ives, New York City

Washington Canapé

Loaf of day-old bread	1 tbsp. butter
Soft butter	2 tbsps. flour
Grated seasoned cheese	1 cup cream
½ lb. flaked crabmeat	Sweet red pepper

Slice bread ⅓ inch thick. Cut into 2½-inch rounds. Toast on one side. Spread untoasted side with soft butter mixed with cheese. (Use equal amount of butter and cheese.) Make a cream sauce of butter, flour, and cream. Add crabmeat and season. Spread the bread rounds with this mixture and bake in hot oven (400°) until delicately brown. Garnish with thin strips of red pepper. Serve hot.

Mrs. G. Edmund Bennett, Katonah, New York

Frozen Cheese

1 lb. cream cheese	2 portions Roquefort cheese
½ pt. cream	1 tsp. paprika
½ tsp. salt	Pinch of pepper
2 tsps. Worcestershire sauce	

Cream Roquefort cheese; add cream cheese; mix well; add cream gradually; add spices and last, Worcestershire sauce. Pack in ice and salt and freeze as a mousse.

Mrs. George Howard, New York City

King David Hors d'Oeuvre

1 long yellow squash (as even shaped as possible)	1 cup of beef, cut in tiny, neat cubes (cooked)
1 cup rice, cooked in a little bouillon	Curry powder to taste

Parboil squash; cut off ends and hollow out, leaving the skin on. Fry 1 teaspoon of curry powder in butter; add meat, rice, and seasoning. Stuff this into the squash. Bake it, basting freely to keep it juicy. Chill and remove skin. Slice like bread and serve.

Mrs. Arthur Tuckerman, New York City

Soups

Clam and Onion Soup

Take 1 quart clams with juice and about 8 good sized onions. Cook in a pot until they are very soft (takes about 2 hours). If there isn't much juice with clams add some water. When they are thoroughly cooked put through a sieve, getting all you can through. Put big spoonful butter and flour into pot. Mix well with salt and pepper and add clam and onion mixture. Then stir in about 2 tablespoons cream.

Lawrence Tibbett

Clam Chowder

1 pt. little neck clams	½ onion
1 qt. soft clams	White of leek (chopped)
Lean pork (sliced)	Celery (chopped)
1 green pepper (chopped)	2 potatoes (diced)
2 tomatoes (crushed)	Paprika
½ pt. double cream	

Put both kinds of clams in a pot with a little water; let them come to a boil. In another pot put pork. Let onion, leek, celery, and green pepper brown over fire. Pour over them the clam broth strained through a fine cloth. Add potatoes (parboiled) and tomatoes. Let mixture boil ½ hour. This soup does not require salt. Add paprika to taste. Just before serving add soft clams and cream.

Mrs. Henry James, New York City

Mrs. George Washington's Crab Soup

1½ cups crabmeat	½ tsp. mushroom sauce
1 qt. milk	½ tsp. A-1 sauce
2 hard-boiled eggs	⅓ cup sherry
Suggestion of nutmeg	½ cup cream
1 tbsp. butter	Salt and pepper
1 tbsp. flour	

Pick meat over for shells, and set aside until needed. Mash the hard-boiled eggs to a paste with a fork and add to them the butter, flour, and a little pepper. Bring the milk to a boil and pour it gradually onto the well-mixed paste of eggs, etc. Put over a low fire, add the crabmeat, and allow to simmer for 5 minutes. Add the cream and bring to the boiling-point again, then add sherry, salt,

and sauce. Heat sufficiently to serve, but do not boil after the
sherry has been added.

Mrs. Franklin Delano Roosevelt, The White House, Washington, District of Columbia

Gilt Edged Bouillon

3 lbs. beef (without bone or fat)	1 cup canned tomatoes
2 qts. cold water	1 small bay leaf
1 piece red pepper pod	6 allspice
1 tsp. salt	1 garlic
1 leek	1 tsp. celery seed
1 carrot (pieced)	1 onion
1 bunch parsley	1 sprig thyme
Cayenne	2 tbsps. sherry
Shell of 1 egg (crushed)	1 egg white
4 cloves	

Put above ingredients in soup kettle, cover, and boil. When boiling
smoothly, set aside where it will simmer steadily. After cooking
2½ hours add carrot, onion, thyme, and parsley. Replace cover,
leaving top one-third open. Boil for 2½ hours. If not strong enough
boil longer. Strain all the broth off through a hair-sieve into a
bowl. It should measure a full quart. Let it stand until next morning and then remove all grease. When clean add sherry, salt, and
cayenne. To clarify bouillon, pour into clean kettle, add unbeaten
egg white and crushed shell; stir these into cold soup until well
mixed. Set it on fire and cook for 10 minutes, let settle and pour
through jelly bag. Do not squeeze bag but allow to drip.

Mrs. Thomas Blagden, Lawrence, Long Island

La Petite Marmite

3 lbs. round beef	3 white turnips
Wings and legs of 3 chickens	3 leeks
½ lb. marrow bone	A few celery leaves
3 carrots	Salt, pepper, spice to taste

Put meat and bones in 3 quarts cold water. Skim very thoroughly just before it begins to boil. Add vegetables, cut in quarters. Season. Bring to a boil, cover pan, and let simmer very slowly for 4 hours. Take off fat, remove bones. Cut up meat and serve meat, vegetables, and bouillon all at once in soup plate.

Gogo Schiaparelli

Jellied Consommé au Caviar

To each cup of jellied consommé add, at the last minute, 1 tablespoon of fresh caviar and top with spoonful of sour cream or fresh whipped cream.

Gladys Cooper

Lentil Soup

Put 2 cups of lentils with a pound of salt pork (cut in pieces) and plenty of sliced onions in a saucepan with 2 pints of cold water. Heat over the fire, add salt and pepper and when it begins to boil, a pinch of soda—not too much. After this, the soup should boil slowly for 3 hours. Serve with croutons fried in butter.

Miss Norma Shearer, Hollywood, California

Potage Velours

½ lb. butter	3 egg yolks
1 tbsp. flour	½ cup cream
2 qts. chicken broth	

Melt ½ of the butter and bind with flour. Add broth and let cook 20 minutes. Skim off. Bind with yolks of egg and cream. Just before serving add rest of butter. Serves 6.

Mrs. Joseph F. Feder, New York City

Swedish Vegetable Cream Soup

1½ cups fresh peas	1½ cups diced carrots
1 cup chopped lettuce	1 cup finely chopped spinach
¼ cup finely chopped leeks	¼ cup chopped parsley

Cook peas and carrots in 3 quarts water for about 20 minutes. Add lettuce, spinach, and leeks; let cook for 10 more minutes. Thicken with 2 or 3 tablespoons of flour stirred in milk; add a lump of butter. Season to taste. Add a cup of cream and the chopped parsley. Serves 6 to 8 persons.

Mrs. Sheldon Whitehouse, New York City

Onion Soup

3 medium-sized onions	2 tbsps. butter
1 qt. clear soup stock	2 oz. grated Swiss and Parmesan cheeses

Slice onions and fry slowly in butter for 15 minutes. Pour in the consommé, stir a little, then simmer slowly for 30 minutes. Pour the soup into an earthen casserole and put one slice toasted French bread on top. Sprinkle with cheese over it. Set in hot oven (400 degrees) to bake for 15 minutes. Remove and serve.

Mrs. George F. Baker, New York City

Cream of Onion Soup

3 large onions	2 potatoes
1 tbsp. butter	1 pt. cream
2 tbsps. flour	Salt and pepper
1 pt. stock	

Cook onions in butter, add flour and stir until slightly cooked. To this add the stock, stirring all the time so it will be smooth. Boil and mash potatoes and add to them the cream. Mix thoroughly and add to the onion mixture. Season and pass through a strainer.

Mrs. Harris Fahnestock, New York City

Pumpkin Soup

2 lbs. of pumpkin	2 tbsps. butter
1 onion (small)	¾ cup cooked rice
1 qt. milk	

Melt the butter; fry out slowly chopped onion until soft. Add cut up pumpkin. Cover with water. Cover and cook slowly until soft. Pass through a sieve. Add milk and rice.

Mrs. Richard Myers, New York City

Mulligatawny Soup

Fry a few sliced onions lightly in butter but do not brown. Also fry ½ apple. Add a little flour and a little curry powder. Add enough bouillon to make it liquid, and enough to cook for ½ hour. Strain. Thicken with yolk of egg. Do not boil after egg is added. Serve the following separately, along with the soup: rings of fried onions, squares of toast, a small dish of dry rice, and slices of lemon.

Mrs. Charles Boyer

Le Petit Borsch

Carrots	Celery
Onions	Tomatoes
Leeks	Turnips
Beets	Juice of 1 lemon
Salt	Pepper
Creamed cheese	1 egg (beaten)

Wash and cut vegetables, especially beets. Place them in pot. Cover with water. Add lemon juice, salt, and pepper to taste. When cooked, strain and serve with small "tartellettes" spread with creamed cheese mixed with one beaten egg.

Tartellettes
Make a dough with ½ pound butter, ¾ pound flour, 1 cup sweet cream, and salt. Roll and cut with biscuit cutter. Before baking smear tartellette with egg.

Madame Igor Stravinsky, New York City

Cheese Soup

1 qt. stock	8 oz. of rarebit or Old English Cheese
1 qt. milk	4 oz. diced carrots
½ tsp. cornstarch	4 oz. celery
½ tsp. soda	4 oz. butter
½ tsp. paprika	4 oz. onions (chopped fine)
2 tsps. chopped parsley	¼ oz. flour
Salt	

Sauté onions lightly, add to white sauce. Add soda, seasoning, and diced cheese. Heat thoroughly until diced cheese is melted.

Mrs. Harold Ruckman Mixsell, New York City

Crême Vichyssoise

2 onions	6 potatoes
3 leeks	2 tbsps. flour
1 qt. broth	Chopped chives
Heavy cream	Nutmeg
Salt	

Slice onions, leeks, and potatoes; put onions and leeks into pan and brown in butter. Add sliced potatoes, flour, and broth. Cook for 40 minutes until potatoes are ready to fall apart. Strain, cool off, and add chopped chives and heavy cream. Top off with nutmeg and salt. Serve.

Jack & Charlie's "21," New York City

Bouillabaisse
(recipe prior to 1800)

½ lb. butter	Meat of small lobster
1 lb. sole (cut in pieces)	1 cup shrimps
10 small clams	10 oysters
1 clove garlic	1 sprig parsley
2 bay leaves	Pulp of 1 lemon
1 tsp. salt	½ tsp. powdered saffron
1 qt. boiling water	1 cup sherry
2 onions (minced fine)	

In a saucepan melt butter, add above ingredients (except sherry) to quart of boiling water. Cover closely and boil for 20 minutes. Thicken if necessary. Add sherry. Pour into soup plates over slices of toast. Serve hot.

Mrs. Reba Holcomb, Newcastle, Delaware

Fish

Tomato and Clams

1 large can Vitelli & Figle long tomatoes	3 tbsps. olive oil
	4 dozen clams
1 can Vitelli & Figle tomato paste	1 tsp. basil
	3 hot peppers

Heat 3 tablespoons of olive oil in skillet. Add tomatoes and tomato paste and cook until thick and stringy. If too thin, thicken with flour. Add basil, hot peppers, and salt to taste. Let simmer until well seasoned. When sauce is almost finished, add clams, which if large have been cut in half. Cook until the edges of clams curl.

Serve this with large dish of dry rice and zucchini (Italian squash).

Zucchini

Slice zucchini in medium slices. Salt, pepper, and fry in oil. Add a little water and simmer until dark.

Duc de Verdura, New York City

Clams Southside

1 qt. clams (hard)	1 small onion
½ pt. cream	Cream sauce
Salt	Dash red pepper

Cut off ears of clams, put onion and clams through chopper. Cook in double boiler 20 minutes. Fifteen minutes before serving add thick cream sauce. Just before serving add cream to thin. When cooked put in oven just long enough to brown on top. Serves 4.

Mrs. Frederic Rhinelander King, New York City

An Oyster Dish

Wrap each oyster in a ribbon of filet of sole, pierce with a tooth-pick, and broil in butter. Prepare the sauce in following manner: Put a large lump of butter in a pan on the stove, brown it, add flour to make a paste, then slowly pour in enough cream to make as much sauce as is desired. Pour this sauce over fresh, finely chopped lobster, let simmer for 3 minutes, then pour over the broiled oysters in the oven and let cook 15 minutes.

Mrs. W. G. Preston, Jr., New York City

Devilled Oysters

1 large onion (chopped)	Hollandaise sauce
4 tbsps. butter	1 tbsp. parsley (chopped)
1 qt. oysters (chopped coarse)	Dash cayenne
½ tsp. salt	1 tsp. Worcestershire sauce
2 eggs (beaten light)	¾ cup fine bread or cracker crumbs

Fry onion in butter, add oysters, salt, parsley, cayenne, and Worcestershire sauce. Boil for 1 minute and add remaining butter, eggs, and cracker crumbs. Stir lightly and bake in a pie dish or a shallow casserole dish about 25 minutes, or until firm and brown. Serve with Hollandaise sauce.

Mrs. Charles H. Marshall, New York City

Oysters in Shells

½ dozen whole-wheat rolls	1 qt. small oysters
¼ lb. butter	Lemon
8 shells	Salt

Grate all of the rolls into crumbs. Melt butter and stir crumbs in it until they are saturated with it. Pick over oysters and drain. Line each one of 8 large shells with crumbs, fill with oysters, and sprinkle with lemon and a very little salt. Cover with crumbs. Bake in hot oven exactly 10 minutes.

Mrs. Thomas R. Waring, Jr., Charleston, South Carolina

Bedspread for Two

6 eggs	Anchovy paste
1 dozen medium oysters	Butter

Stir eggs in a soup plate. Cut up oysters moderately fine in a second soup plate. Rub bottom of blazer (chafing dish) with anchovy paste. Put in good sized piece of butter, and proceed to do eggs into a creamy scramble. Just as they are turning, throw in oysters and stir until well blended and cooked through. Serve on toast slightly spread with anchovy paste.

Mr. Herman Oelrichs, New York City

Crab Stew

4 tbsps. butter	5 tbsps. flour
1 piece red pepper (to taste)	2 cups milk
3 tbsps. Worcestershire sauce	½ cup cream
Segments of lemons	1 tsp. celery salt
4 tbsps. sherry	4 cups crabmeat (shredded)

Cream butter, flour, and pepper until smooth and cook in double boiler. Gradually add milk to mixture and cook slowly until thick. Blend cream, Worcestershire sauce, and celery salt and add to mixture. Add crabmeat and lemon to sauce and keep hot in double boiler. Do not boil. At the last moment, add the sherry and serve.

Mrs. Jay O'Brien, New York City

Crêpes Farcies Rudolf

Cut the meat from a cooked lobster and crabmeat in very small pieces and mix with some light curry sauce and a few chopped mushrooms and truffles. Roll some very fine crêpes with this preparation and serve hot with mustard or curry sauce.

The Colony Restaurant, New York City

Lobster à l'Américaine

Fry 2 finely chopped onions in butter for 2 minutes; add lobster, cut in pieces; add salt and pepper and warm through, leaving on back of stove. Make white sauce with butter and flour, add ½ pint of stock, ½ pint of white wine, 2 tablespoons puree of tomatoes, pepper, and salt. Cover and cook briskly 20 minutes. Then take lobster and arrange on dish; add to sauce juice of ½ lemon and 1 ounce of fresh butter, stir briskly and pour over lobster.

Mrs. Robert W. Lovett, Boston, Massachusetts

Lobster à la Newburg

1 tbsp. butter	2 tbsps. sherry
¼ lb. lobster meat	Yolk of 1 egg
1 pt. milk	2 tbsps. cornstarch

Melt butter in a pan, then add lobster meat. Stir until the meat is braised, about 5 minutes. Add sherry. In another bowl, mix the yolk of an egg and cornstarch. Dissolve this mixture in milk and then add it to the braised lobster meat. Put on a slow fire and let it simmer slowly, stirring constantly. Season to taste. Serve on hot toast. Serves 1 or 2.

Helen Keller, New York City

Rarebit of Lobster

To rich Newburg sauce add 1 cup white sauce for binding and
½ cup of grated American cheese and ½ cup genuine Swiss
cheese. Add 2 cups fresh lobster forced through medium-mesh
strainer. When thoroughly heated add more sherry and seasoning, pour on platter, sprinkle generously with grated cheese, put
under flame, and when cheese is melted and brown, serve at once.

Miss Margot Montgomery, New York City

Lobster Romance

Baby lobsters	2 red pimientoes
French dressing	¼ green pimiento
1 tomato (chopped fine)	Chopped parsley
English mustard	Garlic
Rice	

Boil rice (not too soft). Salt and pepper to taste. Cool. Add red and
green pimientoes and tomato. Make mayonnaise with English mustard, parsley, and hint of garlic. Stir into rice till firm enough to
stand as if taken from an oblong mold. Boil baby lobsters. Remove
from shells and space evenly around rice mold. Place in ice box till
thoroughly cold; serve with French dressing "apart" in a sauce boat.

Countess di Zoppola, New York City

Moules Marinière

6 dozen medium size mussels	¼ lb. sweet butter
8 chopped shallots	1 pt. dry white wine
Chopped parsley	1 lump butter
1 ladle Hollandaise sauce	1 pinch cayenne
Juice of 2 lemons	

Wash and brush thoroughly mussels. Put them in a pan with butter, shallots, and wine. Season with pinch of salt. Cook on stove 15 minutes, then remove from fire. Open mussels and put on platter on their half shells. At the same time let the liquid boil until it simmers to half its former volume. Add a pinch of chopped parsley. Remove again from fire, add a lump of butter and Hollandaise sauce, and mix briskly with a whip. Complete the seasoning with cayenne pepper and lemon juice. When ready to serve, pour that sauce over mussels and sprinkle some chopped parsley on top. Serves 4.

Mrs. James Roosevelt, Hyde Park, New York

Moules Farcies

Heat in a pan 3 tablespoonfuls of olive oil, add 1 small onion (chopped), and 2 leeks (white part only; cut in thin pieces); cook for a few minutes, then add 2 tomatoes (cut in pieces), chopped garlic, a bouquet of thyme and bay leaves, a pinch of saffron, and 2 glassfuls of dry white wine, salt, and coarsely broken pepper. Let all this reduce.

Add mussels (carefully cleaned), put the lid on, and toss them occasionally; they will soon open. Keep them on a slow fire five minutes more, remove them, take them out of the shells, chop them, and mix with the sauce, then stuff half of the shells. When cold, they can be covered with parsley-sprinkled aspic if desired.

Laurence Olivier

Filet of Sole Véronique

6-8 filets	½ cup fish stock
2 oz. dry white wine	½ cup heavy cream
2 tbsps. sweet butter	Seedless white grapes
2 tbsps. flour	Parsley
12 crawfish or pieces of lobster meat	Lemon juice
1 tsp. chopped shallot	

Prepare crawfish or lobster beforehand. Put grapes in a saucepan with enough wine to cover and poach. When ready, place the filets in a buttered shallow pan. Sprinkle with shallot. Pour over wine, fish stock, salt and pepper to taste, if desired lemon juice or pinch of thyme, and parsley. Cover pan with buttered paper and bring to boiling point. Filets should not be cooked longer than 6 minutes. Remove filets and place on serving dish in hot place until sauce is ready. Reduce gravy in pan to ½ by boiling. Thicken with flour mixed with butter or egg yolks, if preferred. (If egg yolks are used, do not add until very last after cream and butter have been added, and do not boil after addition of egg yolks.) Stir well, then add cream until desired thickness is reached. Bring sauce to boiling point again (if flour is used), cover the filets entirely with this sauce, arrange grapes which have been drained around the filets, place crawfish or lobster pieces on top of filets, and put platter under the broiler just long enough to glaze and delicately brown the sauce. Watch carefully. Serves 6 to 8.

Vivien Leigh

Mousseline de Soles Empire

5 soles weighing about 1 lb. each	1 qt. thick cream
1 cup thick white sauce	3 whites of eggs (lightly beaten)
Fish stock	Cayenne
Pepper	Rhine wine
Shrimp patties	

Skin and fillet the soles. White sauce should be made with fish stock seasoned with salt and cayenne pepper. Combine the fish with whites of eggs and thick white sauce, mixing well together in mortar. Sieve and place in a refrigerator for an hour to cool and thicken. Now add the cream, mixing well with a wooden spatula. Form into balls or cylinders (*quenelles*) and poach for 10 minutes in a covered casserole. (The salt water in which the *quenelles* cook should be just under boiling temperature.) Turn out on a hot plate; mask with a white sauce made with fish stock and Rhine wine and garnish with small shrimp patties. Serves 10.

Mrs. Drexel Dahlgren, Philadelphia, Pennsylvania

Sole Pilaff Hollandaise Sauce

Rice

Place 1 small onion (chopped fine) with 2 tablespoons butter in upper part of double boiler. Cook slowly for 2 minutes, add the rice and let cook together a little longer, stirring until the rice is well saturated with the butter. Then add the water and salt and let come to a boil. Place over the under part of boiler and steam for 35 or 40 minutes. The rice should then be soft and each grain well separated.

Fish

Have lemon sole delivered in filets, with bones sent along with it. Cut the filets in pieces, one and a half inches long by half an inch wide. Let soak in cream for a few hours.

Broth

With a little carrot, onion, celery, parsley, and fish bones prepare a strong broth, cooking it only 15 minutes, and strain. Drain the pieces of fish, roll them in flour, and cook in butter to a golden color. Then combine with the rice, proceeding exactly as for Chicken Pilaff.

Sauce

1 heaping tbsp. butter	1 cup fish broth
1 heaping tbsp. flour	⅓ cup cream
2 yolks of egg	Juice of ½ lemon

Combine butter, flour, and yolks of eggs in a saucepan; dilute with the fish broth and cream. When thoroughly mixed, place on slow fire, allow to thicken, stirring all the while, but do not let boil. Add lemon juice and serve. Serves 6.

Mary Cass Canfield, New York City

Mousse of Shad Roe à la Newburg

Shad roe	White sauce
1 egg	Butter
Sherry	Lobster sauce
Hollandaise sauce	Heavy cream
Wild rice	

Remove the skin and crush the shad roe. Bind with a small quantity of white sauce and add a whipped white of an egg. Season and poach in a buttered form. Add sufficient sherry to some lobster sauce, reduce and thicken with a little Hollandaise sauce and heavy cream. Pour the sauce over the mousse. Serve with bordure of wild rice.

Restaurant Voisin, New York City

Trout Marguery

Trout	Salt
3 tbsps. olive oil	Pepper
½ glass water	Hollandaise sauce
½ lb. melted butter	12 lake shrimp
½ can mushrooms	2 truffles (sliced)

Clean, skin and bone your fish, cut in filets tenderloin, roll them, put olive oil in pan with the fish and season with salt and pepper. Add water and bake in a hot oven. When cooked dress on platter. Make a Hollandaise sauce: Take yolks and beat them, drip butter in a double boiler or on a slow fire until thick, add lemon juice, shrimp, mushrooms, truffles and a little water from the fish, take off fire, and serve over fish.

Mrs. David M. Weeks, New York City

Filet of Striped Bass, Bonne Femme

Shallots (chopped)	Salt
Parsley	Pepper
Mushrooms (sliced)	Butter
Wine sauce	Yolks of 3 eggs
Filet of bass	

Sprinkle buttered pan with shallots and parsley and lay fish in pan. Season with salt and pepper and add mushrooms. Sprinkle wine sauce and fish broth over filet of bass. Bake 10 minutes. Place fish on serving dish and pour over it the sauce of the cooking pan after it has been thickened with the yolks and a little butter. Serve very hot.

Mrs. Nicholas Biddle, New York City

Fish Mousse

Fresh haddock	2 egg yolks
1 qt. boiled cream	¾ lb. butter

Clean the fish in running water. Never wash fish after it has been cut, but before, and do not soak fish in water. Dry the fish in a towel and cut in 2 pieces. Remove back-bone and clean. To 2 pounds of fish, add ½ cup of butter and a quart of boiled cream, which has been allowed to cool, and 2 egg yolks. The fish is ground 3 times in a grinder, the last time with the butter. Then pound the fish and put in dish for 10 minutes. Dilute with the sauce until the mousse is satisfactorily thick and firm. Add a few grains of vegetable salt and pepper. The mousse is then smeared with big pieces of butter (sweet) and when the pot of water is boiling the fish is put in it and placed in the oven at medium heat. Cook for 1½ hours.

Sauce

1 can of shrimp	3 tbsps. of flour
1 large cup of milk	3 tbsps. of butter

The head and back-bone are cooked and the stock used for the sauce. Melt butter in a double boiler, add flour, and mix thoroughly, then use 1 large cup of the stock and the milk. A little salt and pepper and Worcestershire sauce are added. Warm can of shrimps and put in the middle of the mousse and pour sauce over it. Serves 6 people. Always use wooden spoon. Lobster may be substituted.

Mme. Jean Des Vignes, New York City

Finnan Haddie with Oysters

| 2 cups finnan haddie | 1½ cups cream sauce |
| 1 pt. oysters | |

Soak finnan haddie for 30 minutes. Simmer until cooked. Flake it into medium-sized pieces. Heat oysters in own liquor. As soon as edges curl put in cream sauce. Add finnan haddie, stir and let simmer only, for about 5 minutes, adding slight dash salt and generous portion paprika.

Miss Daisy Rogers, New York City

Sweetsour Fish

1 fish, medium size	Ginger (fine cut)
1 small turnip (sliced fine)	1 small carrot (sliced fine)
3 cups lard or oil	½ onion (sliced fine)

Cornstarch Paste

| 3 tbsps. cornstarch | 2 tbsps. water |

Sweetsour Sauce

4 tbsps. soy sauce	1 tbsp. cornstarch
3 tbsps. sugar	½ cup water
2 tbsps. vinegar	

Clean fish and make diagonal slashes on each side from tail to head, leaving the flesh adhering to the bones. Smear well with the cornstarch paste. Heat pan, add lard, and let it come to a boil. Fry fish until crisp. Remove fish from pan and drain. Reheat pan and add 3 tablespoons of oil. Fry ginger, carrot, onion, and other ingredients. Cook for a minute. Add sweetsour sauce to vegetables. Boil for a minute and pour over fish.

Pearl S. Buck, Perkasie, Pennsylvania

Swedish Fish Ring

Clean, scrape, split open, and bone 1 medium-sized white fish (pike, pickerel or other fish may be used) and 1 pound salmon. Put both in a wooden bowl and pound very fine or run through meat grinder several times, until meat is like pulp.

Add gradually, while beating, 3 egg yolks (well beaten), 1 cup heavy cream (whipped), 1 cup light cream, 1 teaspoon salt, ½ teaspoon cayenne pepper, ½ teaspoon nutmeg, and last the stiffly beaten egg-whites. Pour into a buttered ring mold. Place mold in pan or dish of hot water. Bake in moderate oven 40 to 50 minutes, until set. Serve hot with the following sauce:

Sauce la Bernadotte

Put a wooden bowl in icebox to be ice-cold. Stir 2 egg yolks with 1 teaspoon salt until thick and lemon-colored. Drip 1 cup oil in while stirring. Stir until smooth and thick. Put in ½ teaspoon mustard, 2 teaspoons lemon juice, ¼ teaspoon white pepper, 1 teaspoon Worcestershire sauce, and ½ cup ketchup. Blend thoroughly in top part of double boiler 1 tablespoon flour, 2 tablespoons

butter; add gradually, stirring constantly, 1 cup light cream,
½ teaspoon sugar, ½ teaspoon salt, and 1 teaspoon juice of
capers. Combine everything together in top of double boiler; heat
but not boil. Boil 1 lobster, cool, cut in pieces; cut 1 can asparagus tips in pieces. Combine with sauce in double boiler; heat
thoroughly. Put fish ring on a platter; pour over the sauce. Serve.
If possible add also ½ glass of good imported sherry in the sauce.

Mrs. John C. Wilson (Princess Paley), New York City

Venetian Fish Aspic

5 lbs. fish	1 tsp. dry mustard
1 carrot	Bunch celery
1 bay leaf	1 onion
Juice of 1 lemon	Salt to taste
½ cup sherry	1 can of green madrilene
Worcestershire sauce	Tabasco (few drops)
Lettuce leaves	Asparagus
Devilled eggs	Shrimp
Mayonnaise	Chili sauce
2 tbsps. thick cream	2 tbsps. chives (chopped)

Clean fish (flounder, halibut, or any other firm fish), but do not
skin. Simmer whole, including the head, adding to pan small
amount of water, sliced carrot, celery stalk, bay leaf, and onion.
When fish is done (about 20 minutes), remove from stock and separate meat into portions, removing skin and bones. Arrange in
fish-shaped mold. To the strained stock add a can of green
madrilene, juice of lemon, sherry, a dash of Worcestershire sauce,
and a few drops of Tabasco. Pour over fish and cool. When ready
to serve, arrange on platter garnished with lettuce or watercress.
Arrange around it piles of asparagus, alternating with halves of
devilled eggs, a fresh cooked shrimp pressed into each egg-half.

Two-thirds parts mayonnaise mixed with one-third part chili sauce, juice of 1 lemon, 2 tablespoons Worcestershire sauce, 2 tablespoons cream, chopped chives and mustard. Serves 10.

Mrs. Nelson Crane, New York City

Fish Timbale

5 lbs. raw fish shredded	5 yolks of eggs
½ loaf bread crumbs	1½ pts. cream
1 tbsp. chopped parsley	1 tbsp. onion juice
2 tbsps. butter	Salt and pepper

Chop fish fine. Add eggs, crumbs soaked in cream, onion juice, parsley, salt and pepper. Pound all together and add butter. Pour in greased mold which is put in boiling water. Boil 2 hours. Serve with cream sauce with shrimp, lobster, or mushrooms.

Mrs. Charles E. Kock, Greenwich, Connecticut

Maine Fish Balls

6 medium-sized potatoes	3 eggs
1 cup pickled salt cod fish	A little nutmeg, salt and pepper
2 tbsps. butter	

Soften fish in water overnight and flake very fine. Peel, boil, drain, and mash potatoes. Mix with fish. Stir in butter and egg yolks. Season and blend mixture well. Beat egg whites and carefully fold into mixture. While still warm spoon up a glob of it and drop into bubbling hot fat. Fry for about 3 minutes, or until it turns to a delicate golden brown.

Robert E. Sherwood, New York City

Frog Legs Sauté Salonaise

10 small frog legs	2 tbsps. olive oil
½ cup heavy cream	1 onion
Salt	½ eggplant
Pepper	1 tomato
4 tbsps. flour	

Dip the frog legs in cream and season. Roll in flour and fry in hot olive oil until golden brown. Sauté onion, diced eggplant, and chopped fresh tomato. Cook for 10 minutes. Pour on frog legs. Serve with lemon. Serves 2.

Katharine Cornell

Entrées

—

Eggs Madras

Fry in butter 1 or 2 good sized onions (sliced), add a dessert-spoonful of good curry powder and fry for a few minutes. Lastly fry and add slices of hard-boiled eggs cut ¼ inch thick (you will want about 2 eggs). Have a Pyrex (or other) flat dish buttered, and lay slices of raw tomato on the bottom. Sprinkle with salt, pepper, and grated Parmesan cheese. Lay the fried eggs and onions over these, then pour over the mixture ½ pint of good velouté sauce, or any white sauce made with butter. Now spread over all a layer of nicely cooked Patna rice and a little fresh cream (if you have it).

Cover the dish with a plate or buttered paper to prevent the rice from hardening, then put it in the oven for about 30 minutes. (Moderate oven.)

Mrs. Louis Paget, Fitzwilliam Depot, New Hampshire

Mushroom Soufflé

Put 1 pound of mushrooms through the chopper; put into a heavy pan, with 1 tablespoon of butter; place the lid on. Cook about 5 minutes; add this to 1½ cups thin sauce containing the usual seasoning and 4 yolks of eggs. Lastly, fold in the 4 beaten whites. Turn into a soufflé dish, standing in a pan of water and pop into a hot oven for 20 minutes. The sauce is made by reducing (rapidly boiling down to half its volume) heavy cream, which is seasoned with a little black pepper, ground from a mill, allspice, and salt.

Miss Harriet McLaughlin, Lake Forest, Illinois

Terrapin

1 terrapin	¾ cup stock
2 slices onion	1½ tbsps. butter
2 slices carrot	2 tbsps. sherry
2 stalks celery	½ cup cream
1½ tbsps. flour	2 eggs
Cayenne pepper	Salt
1 tsp. lemon juice	Toast or puff-paste points

Plunge terrapin into boiling water for 5 minutes. Remove skin from feet and tail by rubbing with towel. Draw head out with skewer; rub off skin. Put in kettle, cover with boiling water. Add carrot, onion, and celery. Cook until tender, about 40 minutes. Remove from water, draw out nails, cut under shell close to upper shell and remove.

Empty upper shell carefully. Remove and discard gall bladder, sand bags, and thick part of intestines. Liver, small intestines, and eggs are used with meat. Cut meat up smaller than a crown piece.

To each terrapin add stock, butter, sherry, cream, flour, and eggs. Dust in very carefully cayenne pepper mixed with salt. Do not add wine and lemon juice until ready to serve. Pour in deep basin and garnish with toast or puff-paste points.

Mrs. Francis H. Janvier, New Castle, Delaware

Gnocchi à la Romaine

¼ cup butter	½ cup cornstarch
¼ cup flour	¾ cup grated cheese
½ tsp. salt	2 cups scalded milk
2 egg yolks	

Melt butter; when bubbling, add flour, cornstarch, salt, and milk gradually. Cook 3 minutes, stirring constantly. Add yolks of eggs, slightly beaten, and ½ cup of cheese. Pour into buttered shallow pan, and cool. It should be about 1 inch thick. Cut in squares and diamonds. Place on platter, sprinkle with remaining cheese, and brown lightly in oven.

Mrs. Cadwallader Jones, New York City

Italian Spaghetti

1 onion (chopped)	½ lb. spaghetti
4 oz. olive oil	1 can bouillon
1 tbsp. butter	½ glass tomato juice
¼ lb. chopped raw beef	1 can tomato paste
½ tsp. celery seed	1 can (small) of sweet
½ tsp. tarragon	peppers, chopped fine
½ tsp. basil	Parmesan cheese
½ tsp. parsley	Salt and pepper

Fry onion in olive oil and butter. Add beef and allow to simmer. When onion begins to brown, add bouillon, tomato juice, tomato paste, and sweet peppers. Chop and mix celery seed, basil, tarragon, and parsley and put into the sauce while it is cooking.

Boil spaghetti 12 or 14 minutes, pour into a colander and rinse with hot water to remove starch. Return spaghetti to pot and pour sauce over it. Mix well and serve with Parmesan cheese.

Mrs. Robert Woods Bliss, Washington, District of Columbia

Frankfurters with Chili Sauce

Boil frankfurters as usual, cut them in 3 pieces, and skin. Melt butter in a pan, add mustard and sugar, and stir well. Add chili sauce and sweet or sour cream; heat but do not boil. Put sausages in the sauce and keep on the stove for a few minutes.

Valentina (Mrs. George Schlee), New York City

Crêpes Provençales

Make béchamel sauce in usual way with butter, flour, and cream. Add 1 tablespoon grated Gruyère cheese. Have ready several slices of ham, chopped very fine. Make very thin pancakes (or crêpes) using flour, milk, eggs, a good pinch of salt, a dash of pepper, and, if desired, a tiny pinch of cayenne. Lay a pancake at the bottom of a buttered baking dish, cover with cream sauce, and sprinkle with chopped ham. Continue process till dish is full; finish pancake with *small* amount of sauce and a dab of butter; also, if desired, an extra sprinkling of grated cheese. Cook in hot oven. Serve in baking dish and cut like a cake.

Princess Djorjadze, New York City

Quick Cheese Soufflé

| 5 eggs | 3 tbsps. grated Parmesan |
| 1/8 lb. butter | or American cheese |

Beat the eggs lightly. Melt the butter in a frying pan, then take the pan off the stove and stir the cheese in until it is melted. If it doesn't melt, put the pan back over the fire, but *don't* let the butter get brown. Pour the mixture into the eggs and beat like mad until you are thoroughly exhausted. Pour the mixture into a buttered casserole or Pyrex dish, and bake in a very hot oven for about 12 minutes, or until it rises over the top of the dish. Eat very hot and very quickly, as it turns into morocco leather in about 6 minutes.

Deems Taylor, New York City

Cold Roquefort Soufflé

4 yolks of eggs	2 whites of eggs
1 tbsp. melted gelatine	4 tbsps. cream
½ pt. sweet cream	½ lb. Roquefort cheese

Put yolks of eggs and 4 tablespoons of cream in a pan. Beat over slow fire until creamy. Add 1 tablespoon melted gelatine and gradually add Roquefort cheese which you have previously put through sieve. Beat ½ pint sweet cream and mix it with whites of eggs beaten stiff. Add it to the cheese mixture and put it in a soufflé dish. Keep in refrigerator 2 hours before serving. Serves 8.

Mrs. Cornelius Vanderbilt, New York City

Cheese Pie

1 pie crust (unbaked)	3 or 4 medium-sized tomatoes,
4 medium-sized white onions,	sliced and dipped in flour
finely chopped	Cup fresh cream
1 box process Swiss cheese	Small can anchovies

Spread chopped onion on crust, then the cheese, then the tomatoes, and finally the anchovies chopped very fine. Pour the cream over and bake in slow oven 45 or 50 minutes. Serve ½ hour after baking.

Mrs. Charles Douglas Jackson, New York City

Southern Spoon Bread

1 pt. cornmeal	1 qt. boiling water
2 tbsps. lard	2 tsps. salt
4 eggs (yolks)	

Scald cornmeal in boiling water. Stir in lard and salt and let cool. Add the well beaten egg yolks and beat thoroughly. Fold in the whites of eggs, beaten until stiff. Place in a well buttered baking dish and bake in a moderate oven for about half an hour, or until well set and golden brown. Serves 10.

Mrs. Frank B. Emery, Cape Elizabeth, Maine

Kedgeree Chafing Dish

6 eggs (beaten light)	1 tsp. onion (chopped)
3 tsps. essence of anchovy	1 piece butter size of egg
3 tsps. Worcestershire sauce	1 salt sp. red pepper
1 salt sp. black pepper	4 tbsps. cream
4 tbsps. milk	

Scramble soft. Have plates ready with hot piece of toast on each. Cover toast with egg and serve immediately.

Mrs. John W. Cross, New York City

Will's Famous Eggs

Take as many eggs as required, breaking each one into a separate cup, and keeping the yolks intact.

Fill a small deep saucepan with bacon grease, bring to a boil. When grease is fairly sizzling, bend pan slightly to one side and slide an egg gently in. A few seconds will cook the white to a nice golden crackly brown; the yolk should be about the consistency of a 3-minute egg.

Remove carefully from saucepan with a wire spoon, thus eliminating grease on plate. (Egg can be quickly basted while in pan to secure uniform cooking.) Serve on toast—or better still—on slices of bread fried in bacon grease.

William Rhinelander Stewart, New York City

Liverburger

Grind uncooked liver. Knead into it a slice of bread soaked in cream. Season to taste with little chopped onion. Drop in spoonfuls into hot olive oil and fry. Serve with crisp bacon and hashed-in-cream potatoes.

Anita Loos, Culver City, California

Meat and Fowl

—

Hamburger

Having satisfied yourself of the social importance of the steer, have your friend the butcher give you a cut of the best Top Round steak.

You chop it at home.

If those among your little group of serious thinkers like onions (most of them do, but few admit it), you chop the *caepa* fine, and mix with the meat. Use salt and black pepper.

Pat the meat into little cakes. They should be firm, but not too closely packed. Fry in fresh butter until crisply browned. Serve at once with pan gravy.

The dish is better than its name!

The eating champion so far uncovered is Bill Paley. It is alleged he consumed eleven at one sitting.

If you wish to inflate your gravy a little add a sprinkling of water, more salt and pepper, and some like a dash of Worcestershire, but, then, the gravy must be served in a bowl.

Herbert Bayard Swope, New York City

Steak Eros

¼ lb. filet steak	1 tsp. Worcestershire sauce
¼ lb. butter	Parsley (chopped)
Salt	Pepper

Beat steak and flatten it out to a very thin shape, salt and pepper to taste. Cook butter in a pan till brown. Add Worcestershire sauce. Cook steak in this, then sprinkle with parsley.

Mrs. Vincent Astor, New York City

Filet de Boeuf Bressanne

Soak a filet of beef (larded) in a marinade of white wine, olive oil, and spices for 48 hours. Roast it in a very hot oven 20 minutes to the pound. Take it out, take off fat, and add a little of the marinade to the gravy. Let it reduce. Add the juice of a lemon and

strain it on a garniture of diced truffles, pistachios, tiny mushrooms, and small olives, which have been previously blanched.
Pour sauce over the filet, let it simmer for a few minutes, and
before serving, sprinkle meat with chopped parsley.

Mary Pickford, Hollywood, California

Steak Diane

Use tenderloin steak. Pound very thin. Use a large pan, copper
pan if possible. Add 2 pieces of butter; when melted and very hot
add chives, Lea & Perrin Sauce, and Escoffier Diable. Then add
salt and pepper and English mustard on the steak before putting
it on the pan. Put the steak on the pan when very hot, quick fire
for about 2 minutes on each side, and pour all the sauce over it.

Lucius Beebe, New York City

Tamale Pie

½ cup oil or other shortening	2 eggs
1 lb. ground steak	2 cups milk
1 lb. lean pork (cut in small pieces)	1 large can tomatoes
2 large onions	1 can yellow cornmeal
1 garlic clove	1 cup ripe olives (whole)

Fry in the shortening ground steak and pork with onions and
garlic until slightly brown. Beat eggs; add milk, tomatoes, cornmeal, and olives. Mix with meat mixture, place in greased baking
dish, and bake in slow oven for 1 hour.

Mrs. Margaret Berr, Tucson, Arizona

Langue Braisée

Brown fresh beef tongue in butter with onions, carrots cut in quarters, and ½ of calf's foot. Season. Add 1 glass of dry white wine. Cover and let it simmer for 4 hours. Skin and serve on platter and arrange onions and carrots around it. Strain gravy through cloth and pour over it.

Lucrezia Bori

New England Boiled Dinner
(with leanings towards croûte au pot)

2 lbs. boiled beef (cubed)	Onions
½ cup horseradish	Peas
½ cup thin cream	Turnips
French mustard	Beets
Parsley	Potatoes
Carrots	

Steam vegetables for 10 minutes, then add to beef 5 minutes before it is ready. Season. Serve with horseradish mixed with cream. Add mustard and chopped parsley.

Albert Spalding, New York City

Russian Meat Loaf

1½ lbs. top round steak (ground)	Salt
1 large onion	Pepper
1 or 2 cups boiled rice	½ cabbage (shredded)
Stock	Sour cream

Remove fat and grind steak. Brown lightly chopped onion in butter and cabbage. Mix this with boiled rice; moisten this with a little stock (or rinse out pan with water and use this). Roll out chopped beef like a pie crust. Fill center with cabbage and rice mixture and fold it in. Place on buttered pan and dot with butter. Bake 40 minutes. Baste with a lot of sour cream.

Alfred Lunt

Lamb Chops in Wine

Brown loin lamb chops in butter with small white onions and carrots. Season. Add ½ cup of dry white wine, and ½ pound of sliced mushrooms. Cover and let cook very slowly for 30 minutes.

Princess Kyril Scherbatow

Yorkshire Hot Pot

Six pounds shoulder of lamb (cut in large pieces); fry in hot fat— add salt and pepper, cover and let simmer.

Boil separately young carrots, small white onions, small new potatoes, and peas.

Take 1 quart of rich milk, 4 heaping tablespoons of flour; mix this with the milk and pour over meat. Stir well, add bay leaves and a bunch of parsley (cooking period of meat—2 hours).

When serving: Put meat in plate, arrange vegetables in groups all around—sprinkle with parsley.

Fanny Brice

Shashlick Caucasian

You take a very young lamb which would not weigh more than 5 pounds and cut off all the fat. The meat from the leg should be cut from the bone in little pieces, of about 28 pieces to a leg. Then take 2 lemons squeezed, 1 glass of olive oil, and a bit of salt and a few grains of pepper. All these are mixed together with the cut pieces of lamb and put in a cold place for 3 or 4 days. Then 15 minutes before you wish to serve, put the pieces of lamb on skewers and broil over charcoals. With this Shashlick you serve rice, lemon, and a sauce called Diable, which is similar to Escoffier Sauce, or an A-1 sauce which can be purchased in the better grocery stores.

Prince Serge Obolensky, New York City

Lamb Kidneys

Lamb kidneys	Butter
Pepper	Orange juice
Salt	Cream (thin)
Hot toast	

Split kidneys; soak in ice water. Grill kidneys in hot sweet butter. Squeeze orange juice over kidneys. Slightly pepper and salt. Last thing stir in thin cream. Serve on hot toast. Pour over sauce from pan.

Mrs. S. K. de Forest, New York City

Veal Kidneys

5 veal kidneys	1 tbsp. fat (butter or bacon grease)
1 lb. mushrooms, chopped very fine	2 tbsps. white wine
1 tbsp. onion, chopped very fine	Salt and pepper

Parboil kidneys a few minutes. Remove skin. Soak in cold water ½ hour. Slice and season with salt and pepper. Cook mushrooms in a little water ¾ of an hour. Cook onions in melted fat for 3 or 4 minutes. Add kidneys to onions and cook 5 minutes. Add mushrooms and cook all together 5 minutes. Add wine and serve.

Mrs. Edwin White, St. Paul, Minnesota

Savory Veal Cutlets

3 peeled onions	2 tbsps. fat
1 tsp. salt	¾ cup sour cream
1 veal cutlet (about 1½ in. thick)	Paprika to taste
¼ cup flour	

Slice onions and brown in skillet with fat. Flour cutlet and brown thoroughly in skillet. Flavor with salt and paprika and add sour cream. Cover and place over very low heat and allow to simmer gently for about an hour, or until tender, turning cutlet once.

Mrs. Charles E. Copeland, Jackson Heights, Long Island

Savoury Rolled Roast Veal

Have the butcher prepare a rump of veal to be rolled, but do not let him roll it, for the cook must first stuff it with the following seasonings. First rub the inside of the piece of veal thoroughly with a clove of garlic, then sprinkle with chopped parsley and a grated onion, dash with salt and pepper, and afterwards smear generously with butter. Then roll the veal and tie with string, and repeat the identical procedure of butter and seasonings on the outside, being sure to have a good coating of butter. Place in an uncovered roasting pan with 2 tablespoons of butter and put in a hot oven till golden brown. At this point, pour a glass of water into the roasting pan; reduce heat of oven to 350°, cover the pan, and cook till done. Then remove to a platter and keep hot while you add to the juices in the pan a tumbler of milk and a small piece of butter. Pour this sauce over the roast and serve with baked string beans and lima beans.

Mrs. Edward J. Mathews, New York City

Blanquette de Veau

Cut veal in cubes and pour boiling salted water over it and let it soak for 20 minutes. Drain it and put in a pan; cover with water. Add small white onions, salt, pepper, a carrot sliced in quarters, bay leaf, and a sprig of parsley. Bring to a boil and simmer slowly. When meat is done make a white sauce with the stock. Let it cook for 20 minutes. Bind it with 2 yolks of eggs mixed with ½ cup cream. Pour over meat and onions and add mushrooms cooked separately.

Mrs. Carroll Carstairs, New York City

Veal with Mushroom Sauce

Small thick pieces of veal	Salt
Butter	Pepper
Olive oil	Cream
Mushrooms	Nutmeg
Milk	

Fry veal in oil and butter until golden. Peel mushrooms, remove stems, peel stems, and cut very thin. Remove veal from pan. Add to juices already in pan a little hot water, 1 tablespoon flour, then a little milk and stir until sauce is brown. Now put in the mushrooms, salt and pepper, and nutmeg (very little). Cook for about 15 minutes on low fire. Put cooked veal into frying pan and add a dash of cream here and there. Heat but do not boil and serve.

Mrs. Fitzhugh Minnegerode, New York City

Daube

3-4 lbs. veal round	1 can tomatoes
Flour	1 tbsp. lard
Onions	Thyme
Chervil	Bay leaf

Half a dozen fresh tomatoes can be substituted for the can of tomatoes. Sprinkle veal on both sides with a little flour. Heat lard in an iron pot. When very hot, fry veal on both sides. Take out, and in that hot lard make a roux. Fry onions, tomatoes, and all the seasoning. When all this is well fried, add veal and the liquid of tomatoes and let simmer 4 hours.

Mrs. J. W. Libby, New Orleans, Louisiana

Jambonneau

Soak pork shoulder in cold water overnight. Put in pan with 1 quart of dry California white wine, 2 onions, 2 carrots, 1 bay leaf, 1 pinch of thyme, whole black pepper, 1 small strip of orange skin, and enough water to cover meat. Bring to a boil and let simmer ½ hour to pound. Take off skin and put back in stock until cold. Take out and roll in bread crumbs. Excellent for picnics.

Philip Barry

Smithfield Ham

(an old Virginia recipe given by Madame Jusserand to Madame Joffre when she was in the United States)

Lay your ham in cold water and, after allowing it to soak for half an hour, scrape and wash it thoroughly. When it is absolutely clean, put it to soak in fresh water and leave it from twelve to thirty-six hours, according to its age and size. Then take a large pot with plenty of water, put in the ham with onions, a little celery, some parsley, two or three blades of mace, and half a dozen cloves. (Any of these garnishments may be omitted, according to your individual taste.) Put the pot on the fire, and as it comes to a boil, skim it well. Then allow it to simmer until it turns over of its own accord in the pot.

When the ham has turned over, which is caused by the gradual swelling of the fat changing its center of gravity, set it off the fire to cool in its own water. Do not let it get cold, but as soon as it is cool enough to handle, place it upon a wooden board and, using a clean cloth, pull off the skin.

Then on the glistening expanse of fat sprinkle a good covering of white pepper. A quarter of a pound is not too much to use on a big ham. Then stud it with finest cloves, pressing them into the fat about an inch apart. Next, take plenty of "open kettle" sugar, the light brown sugar that grandmother used, and put as thick a layer as possible on top of the peppered ham. You can get a sugar coating more than an inch thick, if you work expertly. Then place the ham in an iron pan into which you have poured a pint of good sherry or an equal quantity of fine cider. Put it in a very slow oven, and little by little the sugar will melt through the fat, carrying the pepper and the taste of cloves right through to the bone.

Some of the sugar may run down the sides of the ham into the sherry or cider with some of the fat, but if your oven is not too hot at least four-fifths of the sugar will sink into the ham itself. Towards the end of the cooking, baste the ham with the sherry or cider, and drippings, and it finally comes out a rich dark brown, studded with the "coffin nails of Asia," as cloves were called after the Portuguese had ravished its rich coasts in search of this most fragrant of all spices. There is nothing finer in the world than a slice of this cold ham.

Condé Nast, New York City

Gumbo Filé

1 chicken	Rice
½ lb. lean ham	1 tbsp. lard or 2 of butter
Seasoning	Bay leaf
Thyme	Parsley
1 large onion	3 dozen oysters
2 qts. oyster liquor	2 qts. boiling water
½ pod red pepper	

Clean and cut the chicken as for fricassée; dredge with salt and pepper as to taste. Cut ham in dices. Chop onions, parsley, and thyme very fine. Put the lard or butter in a deep serving pot; when hot put in chicken and ham. Cover closely and cook 10 minutes. Add onion and parsley and thyme, stirring occasionally to prevent burning. Add bay leaf, chopped fine, and pepper pod. Pour in oyster liquor and boiling water. Set back to simmer an hour longer. When nearly ready for dinner and while the gumbo is boiling, add the oysters. Let gumbo remain on the stove for about 3 minutes, then remove the pot from the fire. Add filé to taste. This should be served with rice.

Mrs. J. W. Libby, New Orleans, Louisiana

Chicken Mold — Vienna

Macaroni	Creamed chicken
Sweetbreads	

Boil macaroni in as long strings as possible, 10 to 12 minutes. Pour the water off immediately and stretch the macaroni out on cloths for about ½ hour or until dry. Smear the inside of a bombe form with plenty of butter and line it with the macaroni in a spiral, starting at the bottom. Leave the whole with about ½ inch of forcemeat of chicken. You can then fill the mold with creamed

chicken, sweetbreads, etc. Cover it well with forcemeat. Steam for
1 hour or more. Serve with extra sauce.

Forcemeat

Run breast of 1 large chicken through the meat grinder (raw) 2 or
3 times. Then run it through a fine sieve. Put the bowl in a pan of
cracked ice and beat the chicken. Add the yolks of 3 eggs, salt,
and pepper and beat until very light. Fold in ½ pint cream
(whipped). It is then a light paste and ready to line the mold.

Mrs. Willis F. Harrington, Wilmington, Delaware

A Real Malay Curry

Take 2 fresh coconuts. Save the milk. Grate the whole, and have
1 dish of freshly grated coconut to serve separately. Dampen the
rest with water, and squeeze in a cloth. Repeat several times, to
get as much juice as possible.

Use this milk for cooking your meat, either lamb or chicken, cut
up into not too small pieces. Chicken can be left with its bones,
but skin and fat should be removed from lamb and chicken.

Brown meat in vegetable fat, along with a few shallot onions. Then
place in an earthenware casserole. Any of the vegetables here
described can be added to the casserole, which should simmer for
2 hours. Squash is particularly recommended, as it suggests the
breadfruit often used in the East. Also, an apple or 2 (cut in small
pieces), grated ginger root, 2 bay leaves, a few chilis, potatoes,
and tomatoes. Brown 2 heaping tablespoons of curry powder in
butter until dissolved. Add this to the casserole. Serve. Serve separately 1 large dish of dry rice and small dishes of the following:

plain grated coconut; grated coconut with pimientoes mixed; fried
onion rings; chopped onion and ham; chopped hard-boiled eggs
(yolks and whites in separate dishes); slices of raw tomato; chut-
ney; poppidums (if procurable; fried according to directions on
box); chopped peanuts; and chopped bacon.

Mrs. Arthur Tuckerman, New York City

Tarragon Chicken

Butter	Salt
Chicken	Tarragon
Pepper	1 pt. thick cream

Stuff chicken with tarragon. Put in casserole with plenty of butter,
salt, pepper, and a little water. Cover casserole and cook for 30
minutes, basting from time to time. The chicken being cooked,
take out of casserole, putting in 1 pint or little less of thick double
cream. Stir cream while cooking. Put chicken back into casserole. Carve and serve in casserole dish. Put a little tarragon in the
cream sauce.

Mrs. John W. Cross, New York City

Capon à la Parisienne

1 8–10 lb. capon	1 cup cream
3 celery stalks (cooked)	1 lb. fresh noodles (cooked)
1½ lbs. mushrooms	Butter
1 can truffles	

Roast capon. Cut celery in thin strips. Slice mushrooms and sauté
in butter. Peel truffles and slice. Mix celery, mushrooms, noodles,
and truffles. Add enough butter and bind with cream. Slice filets

of capon and take off bone. Put capon on its back on a platter and fill carcass with mixture. Dress filets on top. Serve with gravy from roasting pan. Serves 8.

Mrs. Joseph F. Feder, New York City

Chicken Pilaff "Cassleigh"

1 small onion (chopped fine)	2 cups of cut chicken
2 tbsps. of butter	Tomato sauce
1 cup (standard) of rice	Salt
2 cups of water	

Rice

Place onion and butter in upper part of double boiler, cook slowly for 2 minutes. Add the rice, and let cook together a little longer, stirring until the rice is well saturated with the butter. Then add the water and salt and let come to a boil. Place over under part of boiler, and steam for 35 to 40 minutes. The rice should then be soft, and each grain well separated.

Chicken

This dish is generally made of left over chicken—roasted or boiled. Have it cut in pieces ¼ of an inch thick and 1 inch long. Have a quart size bowl smeared inside with butter. Place a layer of the rice at the bottom, helping it from the boiler with a 2-pronged fork to prevent mushing. Now place a layer of chicken, and alternate layers until the bowl is full. Press down lightly, cover and keep warm until serving time. Then turn out carefully on a platter.

Tomato Sauce

1 onion (sliced)	1 small can Italian tomato paste
2 tbsps. of butter	Roasted bones from the chicken
1 tbsp. of sugar	Salt
2 cups fresh or canned tomatoes	Paprika

In order to eliminate the objectionable effects of onion and still retain its flavor, it may be parboiled for 2 minutes and drained. Then fry it with butter and sugar to a light yellow color. Add the tomatoes, tomato paste, and the bones. Let cook until it becomes quite thick (about 45 minutes). Remove bones and press through a strainer. Serve alongside or over the chicken and rice.

Mrs. J. Borden Harriman, Oslo, Norway

Paella à la Valenciana

(Spanish rice and chicken)

Chicken	Any fish like fresh cod
Pork	Calamari
Sausages	Mussels
Oil	Shrimps
Onion	Parsley
Garlic	Mint leaves
Tomatoes	Saffron
Green pepper	Red peppers
Valenciana rice	Green peas
Boiling water	Artichoke hearts

This dish is composed of many ingredients. The taste will be richer if all of them are used, but some of them can be omitted if preferred.

Cut chicken, pork, and sausage up small and fry in oil, adding onions, garlic, tomatoes, and green peppers. When well fried, add rice (Valencia preferably). Mix well and add boiling water. Cook the fish separately and add parsley, mint leaves, and saffron. Add to first mixture. Add red sweet peppers and peas when rice is half cooked. Artichoke hearts may be added when everything is well done. This dish is best cooked in an earthenware casserole, not too deep.

Aldous Huxley, Pacific Palisades, California

Chicken Ora

1 small chicken	½ cup Italian tomato puree
1 onion	3 eggs (yolks)
1 tbsp. butter	2 cups cooked rice
1 cup cream	Pepper and salt to taste
1 tbsp. curry powder	

Boil the chicken and cut off white meat and second joints. Slice the onion and fry in butter—do not brown. Put onion and butter in a double boiler; add cream and curry powder and simmer for ½ hour; add tomato puree and cook for 3 minutes; strain, then add egg yolks, well beaten. Put the rice in bottom of glass baking dish, add chicken, and on top pour half of sauce; bake 10 minutes. Serve remainder of sauce apart.

Mrs. Knight Wooly, New York City

Indiana Fried Chicken

Cut frying chicken into small pieces. Mix salt and pepper with flour. Roll each piece of chicken in flour. Heat to sizzling heat butter or lard, only just covering pan with grease, about an inch deep. Fry the chicken crisp and brown on both sides. Cover and cook slowly nearly an hour. The steam makes it tender. Add cream to pan gravy with a pinch of mace and serve with corn fritters or rice cakes. The trick lies in timing of cooking.

Mrs. Wendell Willkie, New York City

Breast of Chicken Hongroise
(cooked in chafing dish)

Select a nice 4-pound chicken. Remove skin and cut out the breast; season with a little salt and sprinkle with paprika. Have ready 4 slices of ham (about 2 slices per breast). Set chafing dish over flame with sweet butter; allow to get hot, then add the breasts, browning on both sides slowly until done.

When cooked remove from chafing dish into a convenient hot plate and keep warm. Place ham in the chafing dish and fry quickly on both sides in the same butter in which the chicken was cooked. Now place the ham with the chicken. In the remaining butter put 1 teaspoonful of paprika and let simmer for a minute; add ¾ pint of thick cream; bring to a boil and reduce to half its quantity. Return the ham and chicken breasts to the chafing dish and again bring to the boiling point. Finish seasoning to taste and serve.

Oscar of the Waldorf

Cold Chicken Garnished

2 roasting chickens	Parsley
Celery	2 tbsps. butter
Herbs	1 cup rich milk
½ cup flour	½ package gelatine
1 cup chicken bone stock	(2 envelopes)
1 cup medium-thick cream	½ cup chicken juice
Peppers	Truffles
Hard-boiled eggs	Tomatoes
1 onion	Watercress

Skin and bone 2 roasting chickens. Boil skin, necks, legs, and giblets together until tender. Add onion, celery, parsley, and herbs for flavor. This takes a couple of hours. Divide the meat into convenient pieces for serving, cutting the breasts into 4 pieces, the second joints into 2 each, if large. The legs are not usually used, but may be. Put in a closely covered kettle and let simmer for about 1 hour with just enough water to cover. Add seasoning during the last half hour. Let stand in the broth to cool. Make a cream sauce of butter and flour. Mix and cook slightly. Add rich milk and cup bone stock. Cook in a double boiler 15 minutes. Dissolve ½ envelope gelatine in cold water. Add to the cream sauce, cool and add 1 cup medium thick cream and half a cup of juice from the chicken. Take out pieces of chicken meat carefully. Set on a platter in the icebox. Put white sauce in icebox but not long enough to set. Strain off the stock from the bones and mix with what remains in the chicken kettle which will not be a quart in all. Dissolve 1½ envelopes gelatine and then add to this. Place this in icebox also. When the chicken is very cold and the white sauce about to set, cover each piece carefully with sauce. Decorate with truffles or peppers. By this time the plain jelly will be ready to set. Line one large plain mold with clear jelly. Let set. Arrange chicken nicely around and pour over it the white jelly. Turn out in a bed of watercress. Put tomatoes or hard-boiled eggs around and serve.

Mrs. Windsor T. White, Cleveland, Ohio

Breast of Guinea Hen Smitane

Wild rice	½ tsp. paprika
Raisins	1 tsp. flour
Guinea hen	Sour cream

Cook wild rice, one part rice and one part broth, for 12 minutes. Sauté the breast for about 10 minutes. Take out of pan, add raisins (cooked for 5 minutes in water), ½ teaspoon of paprika, 1 teaspoon flour, and sour cream or sweet cream. Glacé with rice. Serve.

Jack and Charlie's "21," New York City

duPont Pâté

This recipe came into the family with the marriage of Sophie Dalmas to E. I. duPont in 1791. Whenever Mrs. duPont was in the country, her letters mention sending pâtés to her husband by coach. When they prepared for the voyage to the United States, she made over the mattresses and made up a lot of pâtés. They sailed in October and had a voyage of 93 days, during which provision went bad and gave out, so most of the family lived on the pâtés, except for the baby, who had a nourishing broth made of rats. This pâté is made every Christmas and occasionally for other important events. The greatest trouble is its size. It is made in a thin sheet iron oval pan, 16 inches by 12 inches at the top and 5 ½ inches deep. This serves 75 people.

Crust

1 lb. butter   2½ lbs. flour

Cut the butter through the flour until it disappears. Add 2 ½ full common tumblers of ice water. Knead thoroughly. Beat with a rolling pin, turning and folding, until the dough begins to blister. Wrap in wax paper and put in the ice box for at least 9 hours. Several days won't hurt.

Meats

The sausage meat is necessary, but the rest can be varied, only have proportion of whole meat to sausage about the same.

1 boned turkey	½ lb. boiled fresh beef tongue
1 boned chicken	cut in fine strips
6 boned partridges	2 small cans of truffles diced
or 1 pheasant	6 lbs. fresh veal ⎫ ground
1 lb. salt pork fat cut	3 lbs. fresh pork, ⎬ together
in fine strips	⎭ for sausage

Work up the sausage meat with thyme, 6 bay leaves, cayenne pepper, and salt until it is very highly seasoned. Fry a scrap and taste from time to time. Add the yolk of 1 egg for each pound of meat (9) and season again. If you over season, add more egg, but it must be very highly seasoned.

Butter pan and line with heavily buttered brown paper. Line with crust, saving a small piece for the top. Line this with sausage. Dust all meat with a mixture of thyme, cayenne pepper, and salt and pack in the pan in layers, with sausage meat well stuffed between all layers, also a strip of fat, tongue, and truffles. Pack well. Cover with the crust, with a small hole in the center of it. Let stand for at least 5 hours.

Stand in a dripping pan to catch any overflow and watch that this does not burn. Bake for five hours, covering with paper the first part of the baking.

Stand in a cool place for 12 hours, pour in the meat jelly and let stand for 24 hours. Serve cold.

Meat Jelly

Boil together all bones of the birds including legs and feet to make a good strong stock.

Put in a saucepan 4 ounces gelatine, 6 eggs and shells, 2 tablespoons of salt, rind of one lemon, 2 wine glasses of sherry, 24 peppercorns, 2 quarts of stock. Beat together with an egg beater, put on a good fire, stir until it boils, and boil slowly for 8 minutes. Strain through a cloth until clear.

While still hot, pour through the hole in the pie crust as much as the pie will take up. Let the rest, the larger part, set and serve chopped with the cold sliced pâté.

No matter how awful the meat jelly looks while cooking, don't throw it away.

(Miss) Aileen duPont, Wilmington, Delaware

Squabs en Casserole

Clean and stuff squabs with parsley dressing, and cook in medium oven for 35 minutes, with one strip bacon across the back of each squab. Dab generously with butter, and baste frequently. Pour contents of a can of French peas into bottom of casserole. Mix in 1 chopped onion, slightly sautéed. Place the cooked squab on top of peas. Take the juice in which the squabs have been cooked and add a cup of sliced mushrooms and 2 tablespoons of sherry. Cook this mixture until the mushrooms are done. Then pour into casserole. Place casserole in oven for a few minutes, until peas are thoroughly heated.

Mrs. Allan A. Ryan

Pigeon Pie

6 pigeons	2 cups stock
6 strips bacon	1 tsp. Kitchen Bouquet
1 tbsp. butter	Pepper & salt
1½ tsps. flour	3 onions

Have the pigeons cleaned. Put them in a baking pan with the small strips of bacon on each pigeon. Place them in a hot oven, 500 degrees Fahrenheit, and bake for 5 minutes. Put the butter and flour in a saucepan. When they are blended, add the stock, Kitchen Bouquet, and seasoning, allowing them to come to a boil; then add the onions and pigeons. Push to the back of the range and simmer for an hour. Put the pigeons in a pie dish. Cover them with puff paste and bake in a hot oven, again 500 degrees Fahrenheit, about 12 minutes.

Mrs. George B. St. George

Perdrix aux Choux

Take 4 or 5 slices of salt pork and cook in a *cocotte*, or heavy iron pot, for a few minutes before putting in your 2 partridges. Season well with pepper and a little bay leaf, crushed, and turn the birds till they brown. At this point, slice a small onion thinly, and also a cabbage, and put in the pot along with the birds. When done, dish the partridges on a platter with the cabbage around it. This is one of the most typical French Canadian dishes.

Mrs. F. Higginson Cabot, Jr., Murray Bay, Canada

Old Fashioned Hunting Dinner

Two partridges, wrapped in slices of bacon, to be put on the grill; leave 15 minutes until *half* done.

Cut all meat off the bones in thin slices. Keep bones. Crush bones in a French crusher (used for Canard à l'Orange) or if crusher not available push through meat grinder. Let the juice drip off through a thin towel in order to separate it from crushed bones. Put bacon that was around partridges into deep pottery dish, add pats of butter in between. Put on it:

a – one layer of sauerkraut, already cooked before with a dash of champagne
b – another layer of bacon
c – a layer of the thinly sliced partridges
d – another layer of mashed potatoes
e – sprinkle top with grated cheese and drawn butter

Bake in oven "au gratin" for 20 minutes. Use juice from bones with the juice of sliced onions fried in butter (the onion strained off) for a sauce to which you add pepper, salt, lemon juice (about

½ teaspoonful), 1 pint sour cream, and a full tablespoon Bovril. Serve hot dish and "sauce" together with Salade Romaine.

Miss Mady Christians

Broiled Duckling

Small duck	Flour
Salt	Ginger
Pepper	Butter

Split a small duck. Trim off extra fat and neck. Rub (skin side) with flour and a little ginger. Let stand a couple of hours. Salt and pepper and then broil as you would a chicken. Broil slowly and baste with a little butter now and then. Very simple and very good.

Lynn Fontanne, Genesee Depot, Wisconsin

Canard à la Bigarrade

1 duck	Flour
1 large onion	Butter
1 cup mushroom caps	1 bay leaf
Thyme	Pinch marjoram
Sage	Rind of 1 orange
½ tsp. Kitchen Bouquet	Juice of 1 orange
1 glass sherry	Puff paste
Salt	Pepper

Skin and cut the duck in 4 pieces. Cook duck carcass in water just enough to cover. Flour and fry duck in butter 3 minutes on each side. Then sauté 1 fairly large onion in butter. Add this to the duck, also mushroom caps, bay leaf, marjoram, thyme, sage, and rind and juice of orange. Then pour stock over duck. Salt and pepper. Add Kitchen Bouquet. Cook 1½ to 1¾ hours, according to size of duck. Thicken, then add sherry or port wine, which is better. Serve on platter. Garnish with half moon puff paste and quarter oranges.

Mrs. M. G. Rafferty, Greenwich, Connecticut

Rabbit à la Marengo

2 tbsps. oil	Salt
Rabbit (sliced)	Pepper
1 lb. mushrooms	Parsley (hashed)
Truffles (sliced)	2 tbsps. tomato sauce

Cut rabbit in medium slices. Put oil in saucepan and let heat. When oil starts smoking add rabbit, salt, and pepper and let cook on hot fire ½ hour. Leave saucepan on side of the stove, take half the oil the rabbit has cooked in and put it in a small saucepan, let heat well and in it cook mushrooms, parsley, and truffles; add tomato sauce. When mushrooms are cooked serve rabbit and pour sauce over it.

Mrs. Francis Hallowell, New York City

Filet de Chevreuil

Soak venison filet for 48 hours in a marinade of wine, onions, spices, and herbs to taste. Roast it or broil it 20 minutes to the pound, basting constantly with melted butter mixed with some of the marinade. Reduce the remaining marinade on very hot fire, and add it to the gravy. Bind with yolks of eggs and a few spoonfuls of good mustard.

Noël Coward

Vegetables

—

Pommes de Terre Frites

Peel potatoes and wash in cold water. Dry in clean cloth, and cut in long strips. Fry a few at a time in very hot olive oil (using frying basket) for 5 minutes, stirring constantly. Take potatoes out and let them cool and drain on brown paper. When all have been done, heat your oil to even higher temperature and plunge the basket in it with the potatoes for 1 minute. Drain again on brown paper, sprinkle with salt, and serve very hot.

Clifton Webb

Pommes de Terres au Dauphinois

Potatoes	Milk
Garlic	2 eggs (yolks)
Salt	Grated Gruyère cheese
Black pepper	

Slice potatoes round very thin. Put in Pyrex baking dish with salt and pepper. Cut up garlic (round) quite a bit. Put in with potatoes and add enough milk to soak potatoes well. Beat egg yolks, mix with a little milk, and pour mixture over potatoes. Spread grated cheese over dish and put bits of butter on top. Bake just enough in hot oven, then in medium.

Mrs. Fitzhugh Minnegerode, New York City

Petits Pois Bonne Femme

2 lbs. peas	1 lump sugar
1 small head of Boston lettuce	1 sprig of parsley
4 small white onions	Salt, pepper, bay leaf
1 tbsp. butter	Pinch of thyme

Put ingredients in a pan. When butter is melted, cover and let cook very slowly for 40 minutes. Serves 4.

Mrs. Gurney Taylor, New York City

Baked String Beans and Lima Beans

Boil 3 pounds of fresh green string beans in salted water, and in a separate pot heat up 2 cans of tiny green lima beans. Drain the water off the beans and limas and while they are still hot mix them in a bowl together with a white sauce (made of butter, flour, and milk) to which has been added a saucerful of freshly grated Parmesan cheese. Put the mixture of limas, beans, and sauce in an oval earthenware dish or in an oval Pyrex dish, cover with some of the white sauce which you will have set aside when you made it, and put in the broiling oven under a very slow fire for about 10 minutes, watching carefully that it does not get burned. This serves 10 people.

Mrs. Edward J. Mathews, New York City

Spinach Soufflé

3 cups cooked spinach	4 tbsps. butter
(chopped very fine)	3 tbsps. flour
1½ cups milk	3 eggs
Salt	Pepper

Make cream sauce with butter, flour, milk, and yolks of eggs. Season and add to spinach. Fold in stiffly beaten egg whites. Put in baking dish, set in pan of hot water, bake in moderate oven about 1 hour. Serve with Hollandaise sauce or cook in ring and fill with creamed scallops or any kind of fish.

Mrs. Ivar Bryce, New York City

Tomatoes Emy

4 whole tomatoes	½ cup cream
⅓ cup water	1 tsp. baking soda
2 tbsps. butter	Pinch salt, pepper, and sugar

Simmer everything but cream for 1 hour in an iron pan. Just before serving pour cream over the mixture.

Mrs. Knight Wooly, New York City

Corn Fritters

Take one dozen ears of sweet white corn. Grate them on a large tin grater. Beat 6 eggs lightly and add them with a little sweet milk (not skimmed). Stir in a small portion of flour, making a thick batter, adding some salt. Fry in fresh lard.

Mrs. Raymond Harper, Newtown, Pennsylvania

Corn Pudding

1 dozen ears of corn	2 eggs
2 cups milk	2 tbsps. butter (melted)
2 tbsps. sugar	

Remove husks from corn. Cut down the center of the kernels with a sharp knife and scrape the pulp. To 1 cup of this pulp add eggs, butter, milk, sugar, and pinch of salt and stir all together in a pudding pan and bake in moderate oven.

Mrs. Frank B. Emery, Cape Elizabeth, Maine

Artichoke Sauce Mornay

Put artichokes in boiling water with salt until soft. Discard leaves and barb and keep only the hearts.

Make a white creamed sauce with butter, flour, milk, and cream; flavor with salt and very little pepper. Make the sauce a little thick and make enough to cover your hearts of artichokes. Outside of the fire add grated imported Swiss cheese to your sauce. Put the hearts in a buttered Pyrex dish, pour the white sauce over them, and put in medium oven for 20 minutes.

Mrs. M. J. Frank, Newtown, Connecticut

Creamed Mushrooms

Large mushrooms	Butter
White wine	Meat fat
Cream	Onion

Take large mushrooms, peel outer skin and slice. Fry in butter or meat fat (but *not* bacon fat). Just before serving, pour on ½ cup white wine to 1 pound mushrooms, stirring and adding also ¼ cup cream. (No thickening.) Season to taste. Serve in a dish in such a manner as to have full benefit of the sauce. Some like a touch of onion or garlic in the seasoning.

Miss Helen M. Shope, New York City

Stuffed Mushroom Bouches

6 extra large sized mushrooms	2 tbsps. butter
1 tbsp. finely chopped shallot	2 tbsps. bread crumbs
2 tbsps. finely chopped chicken liver	Meat stock
1 tbsp. finely chopped parsley	Grated cheese

Peel cap, remove stem. Chop stems fine and fry them in butter. Add shallot, bread crumbs, chicken liver, and parsley. Moisten with meat stock and stuff mushroom caps with mixture. Cover tops with grated bread crumbs mixed with grated cheese. Dot with butter on each one and place in greased baking pan in oven for 15 to 20 minutes.

Mrs. Harvey Cushing, New Haven, Connecticut

Zucchini au Gratin

Italian squash	White sauce
Grated Parmesan cheese	

Peel and cut the squash into pieces. Boil in salt water. Drain and put into a buttered gratin dish. Cover with a white sauce made with butter, flour, and milk; sprinkle with grated Parmesan cheese; and brown under the broiler.

Restaurant Voisin, New York City

Eggplant Reno

3 eggplants	1 onion (chopped)
Canned tomatoes	Salt
Butter	Pepper
Bread crumbs	

Boil eggplants. Remove skins. Pass through sieve. Boil enough tomatoes to equal amount of eggplant, having drained off *all* juice. Add onion, salt and pepper to taste, and butter *or* oil and cook over *slow* fire. Mix eggplant and tomato in baking dish. Cover with bread crumbs and fresh butter. Bake in hot oven till brown.

Mrs. Angier Biddle Duke, Tuxedo Park, New York

Creamed Endive

2 stalks endive (for each person)   Grated cheese
Cream sauce

Take about 2 good solid stalks for each person. Wash and cook in
boiling water 5 to 10 minutes. Pour off water and hold under cold
water faucet. Let the endive be thoroughly washed with cold water.
This removes the bitter taste. Make a cream sauce with some grated
cheese in it. Drain the endive thoroughly. Lay in a casserole and
cover with cream sauce. Bake until the sauce starts to brown.

Miss Helen M. Shope, New York City

Endives au Jus

Endives   Beef stock
Pinch flour   Meat juice

Cook endives in salt water until tender. Drain well. Place in line
in flat Pyrex dish. Pour over it a sauce made of beef stock and
meat juice, preferably veal juice, with a pinch of flour. Cook slowly
in oven about 30 minutes.

Mrs. J. Hampden Dougherty, New York City

Laitue au Gratin

1 medium head of lettuce (firm)	Salt
Cream	Béchamel
Butter	Grated cheese

Take 1 head of lettuce per person. Boil in salt water 15 minutes or until tender. Drain very thoroughly by turning upside down. Prepare a good béchamel with cream; add a handful of grated cheese to taste. Pour sauce over lettuce in a heat-proof dish. Add few dabs of butter and broil until flecked with gold. Serve in same dish.

Mrs. J. Hampden Dougherty, New York City

Salads

—

Délices du Jardin

To make it you must have a first rate vegetable garden or a wonderful green grocer as it includes almost everything—the more the variety, the better the salad. But by the same token it is very flexible and almost any of the ingredients except cabbage, escarole, or endive may be omitted. These are essential as they provide crispness and *texture* which the Chinese and French, the two most civilized peoples in the world, both regard as considerations in good food.

Take two green sweet peppers, half a head each of red and of white cabbage, one head of well bleached escarole, one head of lettuce, one head of romaine, six finely chopped small green onions, two bunches of celery chopped coarsely, one head of raw cauliflower finely broken up, one good sized cucumber (crisp not wilted), one bunch of radishes sliced thin, four good sized tomatoes cut into eighths.

For dressing use the usual base of good olive oil and vinegar which is beaten, one pinch of cayenne pepper, one tablespoon of French mustard, two tablespoons of finely chopped chives, one tablespoon of finely chopped dill, one teaspoon of sugar, salt to taste. This should be mixed so that the mixture is fairly thick with only enough vinegar to give it tang. Mix in a wooden bowl rubbed with garlic which is cleaned only by wiping after use with a crust of bread.

The vegetables should be soaked for an hour before using in ice water and the salad should be mixed only a moment before serving. The virtues of this salad are twofold—its crispness, and the variety of flavors which tickle the palate, separately and together, now cucumber, now cabbage, now onion, now sweet pepper, and so on.

Louis Bromfield, Lucas, Ohio

Alexandre Dumas Salad

(his own invention and his favorite salad)

1-inch cube of tuna	4 to 5 tbsps. tarragon vinegar
3 anchovy fillets	1 cooked beet
1 hard-cooked egg	1 cold cooked potato
1 tbsp. olive oil	1 small celeriac
½ tsp. French mustard	1 cooked rampion
1 pickled gherkin	(turnip will do)
3 sprigs chervil	Salt, lettuce leaves,
1 tsp. soy sauce	Hungarian paprika
(or Worcestershire)	

Make a paste by mashing tuna and anchovies. Work egg yolk smooth with oil and mustard and mix with fish paste. Mince egg white, pickle, and chervil and mix all these together with soy and vinegar. Arrange lettuce leaves in bowl. Slice vegetables and put in bowl with lettuce. Season with salt and paprika. Pour the first mixture over it all and toss lightly but thoroughly for about 20 minutes.

Mrs. Drexel Cromwell, New York City

Golden Gate Salad

Place in wooden bowl which has been well rubbed with garlic: small young, raw spinach leaves; baby raw carrots about 2 inches long; and small bits raw cauliflower. Mix well in French dressing and add freshly ground black pepper over all.

Mrs. Samuel Goldwyn, Beverly Hills, California

Richard II's Cook's Salad

(a favorite of the King's, circa 1390)

Nyme parsel (parsley), sawge (sage), garlic, chibollas (spring
onions), leek, borage, myntes (mints), fenel, and ten tressis (water
cresses), rew, rosemayre, parslayre (purslane), lave and wash
hyme clene, pike hyme, pluk hyme small with thyne hande, and
myng (mix) hyme well with raw oil. Lay on vinegar and salt,
and serve forth.

Mrs. Drexel Dahlgren, Philadelphia, Pennsylvania

Sweetbread Salad

4 sweetbreads	6 small white onions
1 wine glass white	Sprig of parsley
Madeira wine	1 pint bouillon
1 carrot, sliced	French dressing

Soak sweetbreads in cold water for 1 hour. Parboil and cool. Put
sweetbreads in casserole with Madeira wine. Season to taste. Add
carrot, onions, parsley, and bouillon. Cook slowly for 25 to 30
minutes. Let cool. Slice sweetbreads and arrange in salad bowl.
Pour French dressing over it. Serve very cold.

Mrs. Joseph F. Feder, New York City

Senlis Potato Salad

With the usual sliced boiled potatoes add finely diced radishes,
celery, onions, chives, dill, green pepper, tomatoes, raw carrots,
a pinch of cayenne pepper, salt, and black pepper to taste. Mix
this with plenty of home-made mayonnaise made only with oil

and seasoned with garlic, pepper, salt, and onion juice. Serve in a wooden bowl rubbed well with garlic and garnish with red and yellow tomatoes and slices of hard-boiled eggs.

Louis Bromfield, Lucas, Ohio

French Dressing

2 cups olive oil	4 tbsps. Widow's Mite
1 tbsp. wine vinegar	2 tsps. salt
1 tbsp. lemon juice	Few grains celery salt
⅓ tsp. pepper	¾ tbsp. sugar
¼ tsp. paprika	1½ tbsps. catsup

Combine ingredients and beat. Allow 2 peeled garlic buds to stand in dressing for several hours.

Mrs. Benjamin P. Bole, Cleveland, Ohio

Bread and Cakes

Wafer Thin Corn Bread

8 eggs	1 lb. sugar
1 lb. corn flour	1 oz. baking powder
1½ lbs. white flour	7 oz. butter (clarified)
1 qt. milk	Salt

Mix eggs, sugar, salt, and butter, then the rest of the ingredients.
Spread on bottom of baking pan, very, very thin, put in oven for
a while in order to harden. Take out, cut with a knife in oblong,
2 × 3 inches. Put back in oven until a golden color is achieved.
Heat oven 400 to 450 degrees. These wafers can be put in covered
tin box and will keep for several days.

Mrs. Albert Gallatin, New York City

Galette

(an old family recipe from France used for breakfast or tea)

1 pt. milk	1 yeast cake
1½ tbsps. butter	1 tsp. sugar
4 cups flour	Eggs
Cream	

Dissolve yeast cake in warm milk and add to milk. Mix ingredients, add all to 4 cups of flour and knead. Cover with a little flour; let stand for 2 to 3 hours. Roll out thin and put in 3 well buttered pie plates. Scatter bits of butter size of ½ walnut on dough. Take 1 egg for each pan and mix with 3 teaspoons cream to each egg. Beat well. Pour into pans and put in hot oven until slightly brown.

Mrs. Theodore Dixon, New York City

Crumpets

1 cake (4 oz.) yeast	1 tumbler warm water
1 egg and a little salt	4 tbsps. wheat flour

Stir in flour until it is stiff. Set to rise at night—in the morning, if necessary, thin with a little milk. Bake quickly on a griddle.

Mrs. Aiken Simons, Charleston, South Carolina

Great Grandmother's Real Cream Biscuits

2 cups flour	1 cup sweet cream (thick)
2 tsps. baking powder	1 scant tsp. salt (smoothed off)

Make soft dough and roll out thick. Cut with small biscuit cutter. Bake in quick oven.

Mrs. J. Dale Dilworth, Salem, New York

Potato Muffins

2 pts. flour	1 pt. potatoes
2 tsps. yeast	

Mix above ingredients all well together with about 1 pt. warm water (if the weather is cold) to about the consistency of stiff muffins. Salt to your taste. Bake.

Mrs. Henry Ridgely, Dover, Delaware

Tomato Muffins

½ cup butter	1½ cups flour
2 tbsps. sugar	2 tbsps. baking powder
2 eggs	¾ cup tomato juice
Pinch of salt	

Cream butter; add sugar, eggs, salt and flour which has been sifted 3 times with baking powder. Add tomato juice (about ¾ cup) to make it about consistency of cake dough, and beat well. Bake 25 minutes in moderate oven.

Mrs. Laurance S. Rockefeller, New York City

Sponge Cake

½ small lemon (juice and grated rind)	10 oz. sugar (granulated)
5 oz. pastry flour	5 very fresh eggs

Beat the yolks and sugar together until very light. Add the lemon. Beat the whites to a stiff froth. Stir the flour and this froth alternately into the beaten yolks and sugar. Butter and sugar the tin, or tins, and have the mixture about 3 inches deep in them. Sprinkle the top with sugar and bake in a moderate oven (to cool oven) for about three-quarters of an hour. Also can be flavored with orange, brandy, or liqueurs. (Ingredients are sufficient for 2 small cakes.)

Mrs. Ian McEwen, New York City

Orange Cream Cake

8 eggs	1⅓ cups sugar
¼ tsp. cream tartar	Grated rind of 1 orange
Salt	¼ cup orange juice
1 cup and 2 tbsps. cake flour	

Beat whites and salt until foamy, add cream tartar and beat until stiff, add ⅔ cup sugar gradually. Beat well. Beat yolks until thick, add ⅔ cup sugar. Beat again, add orange juice and rind. Fold in whites and sift flour over mixture and fold in. Pour into unbuttered angel food tin. Bake 1 hour or longer in oven, 325 degrees. Invert and cool. Slice in 3 layers.

Filling

¾ cup sugar	Juice and rind of 1 orange
3 tbsps. flour	1 cup whipped cream
1 egg	

Mix ingredients together and cook in double boiler. Cool, fold in 1 cup whipped cream. Spread between layers.

Frosting

1 egg yolk	4 tbsps. butter
2 cups powdered sugar	1 tbsp. cream
Nuts	2 tbsps. orange juice

Mix egg yolk and sugar, adding other ingredients gradually. Spread on top and sides, sprinkle with nuts if desired.

Mrs. A. Atkinson, Tucson, Arizona

White Fruit Cake

1 lb. sugar	1 lb. butter
8 egg whites	1 tbsp. grated nutmeg
1 lb. blanched almonds	1 lb. butternuts (skins removed)
¼ lb. English walnuts	2 lbs. white raisins
1 lb. white citron	1 lb. flour
1 lb. crystallized pineapple	1 tumbler whiskey & wine
2 tbsps. vanilla extract	1 lb. crystallized cherries
2 tbsps. rose extract	

Cream butter and flour together, add whites of eggs beaten stiff. Add all the other ingredients (almonds, nuts, citron, raisins, cherries, and pineapple, chopped very fine beforehand) and bake in oven at 275° F. Oven must be *cold* when cake is put in.

Mrs. Aiken Simons, Charleston, South Carolina

Hazelnut Cake

6 large or 7 small eggs	1 cup flour
⅓ cup water	Grated rind of 1 lemon
1¼ cups sugar	Pinch of salt
2 cups hazelnuts (ground)	2 tsps. baking powder

Beat sugar and egg yolks for 15 minutes, add water slowly. Gradually mix in hazelnuts (ground in almond chopper), lemon rind, and flour sifted 3 times with baking powder. Very carefully fold in egg whites beaten just stiff enough to hold up in peaks. Bake in springform in medium oven (350°) for 50 to 60 minutes.

Cake can be filled or served whole with rum or chocolate icing, as preferred. To fill, split cake with a *sharp long* knife and fill with whipped cream slightly sweetened and flavored with 2 tablespoons rum. Ice with plain butter-rum icing or plain chocolate-butter icing, spread thinly.

Miss Edyth McCoon, New York City

Oatmeal Cakes

2 tbsps. butter	1 cup sugar
Yolks of 2 eggs (beaten)	2½ cups Quaker oats
2¼ level tsps. baking powder	½ tsp. salt
Whites of 2 eggs	1 tsp. vanilla

Beat butter, mixing in gradually ½ cup sugar. Select large eggs and add the beaten yolks, beaten again with ½ cup sugar. Stir in oats mixed with baking powder and salt. Flavor with vanilla. Fold in whites, beaten dry. Drop with a teaspoon on buttered baking dish, making little rounds about 3 inches apart. Bake in slow oven.

Mrs. Alfred Pell, New York City

Almond Cookies

½ lb. almond paste	1 egg white (unbeaten)
1 tsp. vanilla	½ lb. granulated sugar
½ tsp. almond extract	2 egg whites (beaten stiff)

Beat almond paste till smooth, then gradually mix with the sugar till fine. Add the unbeaten egg white and flavorings. Mix all together, lastly add the 2 beaten egg whites. Drop by teaspoonfuls on a well greased cookie sheet, wide apart. Bake in fairly moderate oven 12 to 15 minutes. Before putting cookies in oven, sprinkle with chopped almonds.

Mrs. M. G. Rafferty, Greenwich, Connecticut

Cookies

2 cups flour	2 raw egg yolks
½ cup sugar	1 tsp. vanilla
1 cup butter	1 tsp. brandy
2 cooked egg yolks	

Cream butter, then add gradually sugar and beat. Put egg yolks through a strainer and add to above; mix raw egg yolks with flour and add to foregoing; then add vanilla and brandy. Either put through cookie syringe in forms or cut out, after rolling thin, with cookie forms.

Mrs. Samuel Dushkin, New York City

Scotch Shortbread Cookies

2 cups flour	½ cup powdered sugar
1 cup butter	

Mix all together until you form a soft dough. Roll out about ¼ inch thick and cut with fancy cutter. Bake in moderate oven about 10 minutes. Cool on tray and dust with powdered sugar.

Miss Betty Parker, New York City

Oatmeal Cookies

1 cup oatmeal	¼ cup brown sugar
¼ cup butter	1 tsp. vanilla
Pinch of salt	Chopped nuts
1 tsp. baking powder	

Cream butter and sugar; add oatmeal and other ingredients. Drop by spoonful on to a well greased tray and bake in a moderate oven 10 to 12 minutes. Remove when warm to a wire tray.

Mrs. M. G. Rafferty, Greenwich, Connecticut

Chocolate Cookies

½ cup shortening	½ tsp. salt
¾ cup brown sugar	1 tsp. vanilla
¾ cup granulated sugar	1 cup grated unsweetened
2 eggs	chocolate
2 cups flour	1 cup chopped nuts
1 tsp. baking powder	

Cream shortening and sugar. Add well beaten eggs. Beat this mixture thoroughly. Sift dry ingredients. Stir into creamed mixture. Add vanilla and stir in nuts and grated chocolate. Stir just enough to blend mixture. Drop by teaspoonful on greased cookie sheets. Bake 8 to 10 minutes in oven at 375° F.

Mrs. Harold Hannum, Kennet Square, Pennsylvania

Desserts

Pan Cakes

2 heaping cups flour	2 cups milk
Scant tsp. salt	2 eggs
1½ tsps. baking powder	2 tbsps. butter (melted)

Beat with egg beater and cook on hot griddle. Turn cakes when they make eyes through batter.

Recipe from my father's cook in Maryland.

Miss Helen Hayes

Sour Cream Hot Cakes

2 cups sour cream	1 tsp. salt
2 eggs	¾ cup flour
1 tsp. soda	

Stiffly beat egg whites, add yolks. Beat together; then add sour cream, soda, and salt. Beat all together and add flour. This makes about 30 small pancakes.

Charles Chaplin, Hollywood, California

Crêpes Susette

3 whole eggs	1 cup flour
1 cup milk	Pinch of salt

Beat eggs thoroughly, mix in flour little by little, add milk, and continue to beat mixture.

Sauce

Peel of 2 oranges cut very fine	1 tbsp. butter
Juice of 1 orange	2 tbsps. sugar

Melt butter, mix in sugar and orange juice. Heat peel in mixture. Put small portion of sauce in each pancake before rolling it up. Place in dish for serving, pour brandy over whole. Light brandy, and serve flaming.

Mrs. William Randolph Hearst, New York City

Banbury Tarts

Roll out puff and cut the desired size. An ordinary saucer about 5 inches in diameter can be used, cutting around with a knife. Place the filling on one side of this circle and fold the other side over, moistening the edges with cold water and pressing them all together. With a tined fork mark around the edges. This helps hold them together. An ordinary silver fork will not do, use either a 3- or 4-tined kitchen fork. Prick 3 times on top to let out steam. Arrange on a baking dish, and bake in a moderate oven enough to brown them after they swell to their full size.

Filling for Tarts

1½ cups seeded raisins	1 cup sugar
1 grated lemon rind and juice	½ cup nuts
1 egg	

Put raisins and nuts through meat chopper, add egg beaten slightly, sugar, and lemon rind and juice. Let this mixture stand several hours before using.

Mrs. Christopher Ward, Grenville, Delaware

Salamander Pudding

1 qt. heavy cream	Tiny pinch of salt
8 egg yolks	½ tsp. of vanilla
½ cup of sugar	1 cup brown sugar

Put cream in double boiler, then add the well beaten egg yolks with the salt and sugar and stir until it coats the spoon which takes only a few minutes. Add vanilla. Take off stove, beat for 2 to 3 minutes with an egg beater and put into fireproof dish. Set into pan with ice-water. Do this about 6 hours before serving time to give it a chance to get set.

Just before serving put 1 cup of brown sugar through a fine sieve and spread thickly over the top of the cream.

Brown slightly over low broiler flame or in hot oven.

Mrs. William H. Vanderbilt, Newport, Rhode Island

Hominy Pudding
(old Ridgely recipe for Thanksgiving dinner)

½ lb. butter	8 eggs
1 lemon (rind and juice)	Sugar
1 glass French brandy	Hominy

When your hominy is nearly done boiling, take out a quart of the liquor. When hot add ½ pound butter, eggs, and the grated rind and juice of lemon; sweeten to taste with powdered loaf sugar. Before baking add wine-glass of brandy. Bake in pie crust (use no upper crust).

Mrs. Henry Ridgely, Dover, Delaware

Gentleman's Pudding

Weight of 2 eggs in butter and flour	3 tbsps. raspberry jam
Weight of 1 egg of castor sugar	½ tsp. bicarbonate of soda

Beat butter and sugar to a cream, add flour and eggs, one at a time. Beat well. Then add jam and bicarbonate of soda; butter a basin and steam mixture for 2 hours. Serve with following sauce:

Sauce

2 yolks of eggs   1 good glass sherry
1 tbsp. sugar

Whip to a froth over hot water, add quantity of raspberry jam and serve hot around pudding. (Any jam will do and cream may also be served with it.)

Mrs. Cole Porter

Treacle Pudding

12 oz. flour   1½ lbs. Golden Syrup
6 oz. finely chopped beef suet   Pinch of salt
1 tsp. baking powder

Mix all the dry ingredients to a stiff paste with a little cold water. Roll out in very small rounds (the size of basin required). Put in a layer of beef suet paste and a layer of syrup (slightly warmed) alternately. Tie firmly down and boil for 2 hours.

Countess of Abingdon, London, England

Pineapple Sherbet

1 large pineapple   ½ cup honey
Juice of 2 lemons

Pare pineapple and grate fine. Cook for about 10 minutes in ½ cup honey and 1 quart of water. Strain and let cool. Freeze about 6 minutes in ice cream freezer. Serve with a little fresh pineapple or whipped cream.

Miss Elizabeth Arden

Malay Ice Cream

1 cup guava jelly	2 qts. thick cream
½ cup dry sherry	Juice of 1 lime

Melt jelly with sherry. Add the lime juice and stir into cream. Do not beat. Freeze and serve in glasses. If desired, fresh coconut can be sprinkled over the top before serving. (To melt the jelly, put it into a double boiler with the sherry and let it slowly melt.)

From "The Whole World & Co."

Crème Brûlée

1½ pts. fresh cream	½ lb. granulated sugar
9 yolks of eggs	

Put the cream into a pan and put on the stove to boil; have ready the yolks of eggs mixed with a tablespoonful of the sugar. When the cream comes to the boil add the eggs and make into a custard. When the custard is made, strain into a shallow dish and bake for about 10 minutes until thoroughly set, then take it from the oven and let it cool for 15 minutes. Sprinkle the remainder of the sugar over the custard on top to form a crust; have ready hot salamander and hold it over the sugar to burn it a rich, golden brown. Then put it into a cold place to get thoroughly cold before serving. The burnt crust ought to be crackly, like thin toffey.

Mrs. Paul G. Pennoyer, New York City

Mont Blanc

2 lbs. chestnuts	Sugar
Butter	Chocolate sauce
Cream	

Take chestnuts and put them in cold water. Place them on a fire for ½ hour and peel them while hot. Pass the chestnuts through a strainer. Once strained put in saucepan with butter, cream and sugar. Reheat for short time stirring all the while. Again pass through strainer directly on a platter. Decorate with whipped cream on top or around the dish. Place platter in icebox and serve with hot chocolate sauce.

Mrs. Francis Hallowell, New York City

Pots de Chocolat

| 1 lb. bar sweet chocolate | 4 eggs |
| ¼ pt. milk | ½ pt. cream |

Break up the chocolate. Put it in a pan on moderate fire and stir with wooden spoon adding milk till mixture is absolutely smooth. Stir your yolks of eggs thoroughly and add to chocolate. Let this cook 10 minutes, stirring continually. Then remove from stove to cool. Beat 3 egg whites to snow, then add to cool chocolate and stir well (this is done away from stove). Then add cream. Pour mixture in small pots and put in icebox overnight.

Mrs. Howard Dietz, New York City

Charlotte Russe

2 dozen lady fingers   Sugar
1 qt. cream   6 *marrons*

Line a melon mold with lady fingers. Whip up a quart of cream
and sugar to taste. Mash *marrons* with their sauce and put in with
whipped cream and place in mold and press down as hard as you
can. Then cover top with lady fingers and put in ice box for 3 to 4
hours. Take out of mold and decorate with more *marrons* and their
sauce over it.

Mrs. Drexel Dahlgren, Philadelphia, Pennsylvania

Coffee Pie

Place ½ cup strong coffee and 18 marshmallows in double boiler.
Cook until melted. Remove from heat and beat with rotary beater.
Add ½ tablespoon salt and ½ tablespoon vanilla. Chill until
thick and syrupy. Whip again for an instant and add ⅔ pint stiffly
whipped cream, fold together until smooth and even. In bottom of
a deep pie dish put crumbled coconut cake about an inch and a
half deep and moisten with strong coffee until sticky but not too
wet. Put creamy coffee mixture over it and set in refrigerator.
When ready to serve put minced nuts on top.

Miss Constance Collier

Pecan Pie

1 cup syrup	1 cup pecans (broken)
3 eggs	1 tsp. vanilla
Melted butter (size of egg)	Pinch of salt
¾ cup brown sugar	

Beat eggs, add sugar, syrup, butter, pecans, and vanilla. Put in unbaked pie shell and bake slowly 30 minutes or until set when tried as custard. Serve cold with whipped cream on top.

Mrs. Joseph Waring, Charleston, South Carolina

Les Schenkele

½ lb. powdered sugar	¼ lb. chopped almonds
4 eggs	¼ lb. melted butter
1 liqueur glass brandy	1 lb. flour
Cinnamon	

Mix powdered sugar, almonds, eggs, melted butter, and brandy. Stir it together and add gradually flour to make a thick dough. Work it until it is very smooth and roll it. Cut it in strips and fry in very deep fat until golden (about 4 minutes). Drain on paper and when they are still hot, roll them in powdered sugar mixed with cinnamon.

Recipe from an Alsatian refugee, sent by Miss Anne Morgan

Almondrado
(a Mexican dessert)

6 egg whites	12 tsps. sugar
2 tsps. gelatine	½ tsp. almond flavor
¼ cup cold water	1 cup almonds (blanched
¾ cup boiling water	and ground)

Beat egg whites; soak gelatine in cold water. Add boiling water to fill cup. Add slowly to beaten egg whites. Add to this very slowly the sugar, beating well; add flavoring and almonds. Set in refrigerator or icebox to mold.

Mrs. Margaret Berr, Tucson, Arizona

Gougloff aux Fruits

1 large coffee cake (with raisins)	Cointreau, kirsch, or brandy
1 jar apricot jam	Butter and dried fruit

Slice coffee cake and fry in butter. Mix jam and liqueur and let simmer over low fire for 10 minutes. Add fruits and keep simmering for a few more minutes. Put slices together again to mold to original shape and pour sauce in the center.

Mrs. M. J. Frank, Newtown, Connecticut

Soufflé aux Fruits

½ pt. milk	1 tbsp. flour
¼ cup sugar (granulated)	2 egg yolks
Vanilla	6 egg whites
Candied fruit	

The fruit should be marinated, soaked in kirsch or maraschino wine. Add sugar and vanilla to milk and bring to a boil. Add flour mixed with small quantity of cold milk, and cook for 2 minutes. Take off fire and add yolks of eggs. Let cool, then mix with whites of eggs beaten stiff. Butter a mold and sprinkle it with sugar. Fill it ¾ full with mixture and fruit marinated in kirsch or brandy. Sprinkle with confectioner's sugar and bake in hot oven.

Mrs. H. G. Fairfield, Boston, Massachusetts

Greek Oranges

Pare off the exterior rind (colored part of the skin) of 6 fine navel oranges. Cut these shavings into julienne strips and throw into boiling water for half an hour, changing water 3 times so they will not be bitter. (The water must be boiling each time it is poured on.) As for the oranges themselves, cut off all the soft white under-skin and then halve them, or take the pulp out in sections if you prefer. Now make a sugar syrup (a pound of sugar, sufficient water, and a little red coloring) and boil it for 10 minutes. While it is still boiling, pour it over the orange sections or halves which have been placed in a dish. Let this stand for 15 minutes, then pour off the syrup and boil it again for a quarter of an hour. Finally, cover the oranges again with the syrup, add the julienne of boiled orange peel, cool, and serve. The result justifies these somewhat meticulous directions.

Mrs. Daniel de Menocal, Boston, Massachusetts

Persian Lime Soufflé

3 egg yolks	Juice of 2 or 3 limes
Rind of 1 lime	½ cup sugar
3 egg whites (beaten very stiff)	Green vegetable coloring

Beat yolks until thick and lemon colored. Beat in sugar gradually. Add lime juice, rind, and a few drops green coloring. Fold in egg whites, bake 20 minutes in moderate hot oven—375° F.

Mrs. Ethelbert Warfield, New York City

Molasses Soufflé

3 tbsps. butter	½ cup molasses
4 tbsps. flour	¼ tsp. ginger
4 eggs	¼ tsp. cinnamon
2 tbsps. sugar	Pinch salt
¾ cup of milk	

Melt the butter, add flour and stir. Add milk gradually, stirring well between each addition. Add salt, spices, and molasses and allow to cool. Beat egg yolks and sugar until thick and add to mixture. Last, fold in beaten whites, turn into buttered baking dish, and bake at 325 degrees F. for 50 minutes. Serve with the following sauce:

2 eggs	½ pt. of cream
½ cup of sugar	Rum or cognac brandy

Beat eggs and sugar together until light. Add cream beaten until really stiff. Flavor with rum or cognac brandy, chill, and serve with soufflé.

Miss Gladys Swarthout

Bananas Flambées Kirsch

1 tsp. sweet butter	2 bananas (split lengthwise)
1 tsp. sugar	½ cocktail glass kirsch

When you sit down to luncheon, have cook put bananas in copper saucepan in which there is butter. Sprinkle sugar, cover and let simmer over a very *low* fire while lunch is being served. When plates are changed, cook must throw kirsch over bananas and set it on fire, shake pan until fire dies out, repeat and serve. Portion serves 2.

Mrs. Douglas Ives, New York City

Pommes Flambées au Calvados

Apples	Liqueur Calvados Cusinier
1 tsp. sweet butter	Whipped cream (slightly sweet)
1 tsp. sugar	

Cut apples in quarters. Do as for Bananas Flambées, substituting liqueur. With it, in a bowl, serve separately whipped cream.

Mrs. Douglas Ives, New York City

Charlotte à l'Alsacienne

2 lbs. apples	½ lb. sugar
Cinnamon	Boiling milk
1 lb. white bread	1 oz. sweet butter
2 oz. sugar (granulated)	2 tbsps. kirsch
3 yolks of eggs	½ lb. chopped almonds
3 whites of eggs	Bread crumbs

Peel and core the apples. Slice them very fine and macerate in sugar. Add a little cinnamon. Pour boiling milk over the white bread, cover and let soak for a few minutes. Drain off milk and add sweet butter, granulated sugar, kirsch, yolks of eggs, chopped almonds, the apples, and, last of all, the 3 whites of eggs beaten stiff. Butter a mold, sprinkle it with fine bread crumbs. Pour mixture in it and cook for 1 hour in hot oven. The same can be used with cherries or blueberries instead of apples.

Recipe from an Alsatian refugee, sent by Miss Anne Morgan

Wine Jelly

½ box gelatine	½ cup brandy
1 cup cold water	1 qt. boiling water
Rind of ½ lemon	1½ lemons (juice of)
¾ cup sugar (granulated)	½ cup sherry

Soak gelatine in cold water for ½ hour. Add boiling water, lemon juice and lemon rind, sugar, sherry, and brandy. Place in mold in refrigerator to harden.

Miss Elizabeth Draper, Wilmington, Delaware

Pêches Pochées Princessa Margaretha
(as prepared for Princess Margaretha of Denmark
by Ekegårdh of the Operakallären Restaurant, Stockholm)

Poach your fresh, ripe, white peaches, one to each person, in slightly sugared boiling water, with a piece of vanilla bean, for 6 to 8 minutes. Remove with ladle, take the skins off and keep warm in a little of the liquid.

Get ready a chafing dish, or put a thick pan on the stove. In this put a teaspoon for each person of the following: green-gage-plum preserve, the best procurable red-currant jelly (preferably Bar-le-Duc), and strawberry jam. Heat all 3 together; put in your peaches, pour on brandy and kirsch (about 2 tablespoons of each to each person), do not stir, but heat through, then set alight. Meantime, a serving of vanilla ice-cream has been put on each plate. On each, a peach and a portion of flaming sauce is ladled; sprinkle a few toasted and grated (or sliced) almonds over and serve immediately. Note: This is a spectacular and not too difficult dish to finish in the dining room over an alcohol lamp.

Mrs. James B. Mabon, Jr., New York City

Drinks

Sauternes Punch

2 bottles Sauternes
1 bottle sparkling water
1 box raspberries, lemon
and orange peel

1 small wine glass of
Framboise d'Alsace
(white raspberry brandy)

Place the raspberries, the rind of 1 lemon and of 1 orange in a bowl. Add a very little sugar and pour on enough wine to cover. Add a teaspoonful of the Framboise. Allow this to marinate for about 1 hour. Remove the lemon and orange peel. Put a large chunk of ice in the bowl. Add the remaining wine and Framboise and, at the last minute, the sparkling water. A few sprigs of mint may be added if desired.

Paul Stevenson, New York City

Champagne Punch

1½ ponies brandy	1 pony Benedictine
1 pony maraschino	¼ siphon
Ice	Fruit

To each bottle wine add the above ingredients. Allow 6 to 8 hours for the fruit to marinate in liqueurs. When ready to serve punch, place large block of ice in bowl. Add wine, fruit, and soda. Stir well and decorate with mint.

Miss Anne Morgan, New York City

Tea Punch

2 qts. green tea, *weak*	2 qts. white wine
1 qt. Jamaica rum	1 pt. brandy
Juice of 3 lemons	3 oranges (with peel) in slices

Pour *hot* tea on oranges, add the rest when cold. Serve *very* cold with a few pieces of ice in the bowl.

Cecil Beaton, London, England

Egg Nog

6 eggs	6 tbsps. sugar
¼ pt. Bourbon whiskey	1 pt. cream

Whip cream; whip whites of eggs and yellow separately; add sugar to the yolks; add whiskey little by little to the beaten yolks (it is very important to add whiskey slowly); add cream; and last beat in whites of eggs. Put in icebox and serve very cold with grated cinnamon on top.

Mrs. Harrison Williams, New York City

Cooper River Punch

10 lemons	½ pt. peach brandy
1 pt. brandy	1 gill maraschino
1 lb. rock candy	1 bottle maraschino cherries
1 pt. green tea	2 bottles club soda
1 bottle champagne	

Pare thin the yellow skins of 6 lemons. Steep them in brandy for 3 days. Dissolve rock candy in hot tea—allow to become cold. Then add peach brandy and maraschino or other cordial. Mix the above with your stock and divide in 2 parts. Keep in well corked bottles. When ready to serve, place a block of ice in punch bowl, add 4 sliced lemons, bottle of maraschino cherries, put in ½ your stock—add club soda, champagne. If not sweet enough, add a little rock candy syrup.

Mrs. Aiken Simons, Charleston, South Carolina

May Bowl

A handful of fresh or a large bunch of dried woodruff is tied in a small cheesecloth bag and put into a bowl. Pour over this 2 bottles of American Moselle, or Rhine or Alsatian type wine that has been chilled. Cover and allow to stand for ¾ of an hour. Remove the little bag containing woodruff, squeezing well; add 3 table-spoonfuls of sugar and chill thoroughly. Add 1 pint of fresh strawberries which have been cleaned and hulled. Just before serving, pour over big lump of ice in punch bowl, adding 3 more bottles of chilled wine and sweetening if necessary.

Wine and Food Society, New York City

Fish House Punch

¾ lb. lump sugar	1 qt. cognac
1 qt. lemon juice	2 qts. water
2 qts. Jamaica rum	1 oz. peach brandy

Dissolve sugar in water. When entirely dissolved, add the juices, rum, etc. Put a big lump of solid ice in the punch bowl and allow the mixture to brew for about 2 hours, stirring occasionally.

This punch was concocted by Captain Samuel Morris, first Captain of the Philadelphia City Troop, and first Governor of the State, in Schuylkill, now the famous Fish House Club.

G. Clymer Brooke, Pottstown, Pennsylvania

Le Café Brûlot Diabolique

6 cloves	4 lumps sugar
1 cinnamon stick	4 demi-tasses of strong
4 oz. good brandy	coffee (black)
Skin of ½ lemon	

Put all ingredients except coffee in a *café brûlot* bowl. Set the brandy on fire and stir for 1 or 2 minutes. Add hot coffee slowly and mix thoroughly.

Antoine's, New Orleans, Louisiana

A New Bouquet of Recipes

———

Brioche

1 cup scalded milk	¼ cup lukewarm water
⅔ cup butter	4 well beaten eggs
2 tsps. salt	4½ cups bread flour
½ cup sugar	Melted butter
2 yeast cakes	

Scald the milk and add butter, salt, and sugar, stirring until the butter dissolves. Cool. Dissolve the yeast in lukewarm water and add beaten eggs. Combine the first mixture. Sift flour before measuring and then add to the mixture, beating the dough well. Cover with a cloth and allow to rise for about 6 hours in a warm place. Fill well greased muffin pans about one-third full with dough.

Brush tops with melted butter and let rise for 30 minutes. Bake in hot oven (425 degrees) for 20 minutes.

Lily Pons, New York City

Quiche à la Lorraine

1 pt. light cream	4 eggs
4 slices bacon (fried crisp)	Chives and parsley (chopped fine)
or 2 slices ham (fried crisp)	Salt, pepper, nutmeg to taste
½ onion minced and cooked	A cooked pastry shell (puff paste,
in butter	if possible, in a pie tin)

Heat the cream to boiling and stir, trying to avoid making bubbles, into the slightly beaten eggs. Add cooked onion, parsley, chives, and seasoning. Scatter the crisp ham or bacon, broken in small pieces, on the empty pastry shell, pour in the custard, and bake in a 325 degree oven until set. A few thin slices of Swiss cheese may be used in addition to, or as a variant for, ham or bacon.

Clare Boothe Luce, New York City

Omelet Pavillon

12 eggs	1 egg yolk
2 fresh tomatoes	½ cup Parmesan cheese
2 breasts of chicken (chopped)	1 tbsp. sherry wine
¾ cup of milk	Salt and pepper to taste
¼ lb. of butter	

Beat the eggs with salt and pepper to taste; add tomatoes, peeled and stewed in butter. Prepare sauce with ⅛ pound butter, and 2 tablespoons flour and cook 5 minutes. Add milk, stir until boiling point, seasoning with salt and pepper, allow to cook 15 minutes.

In separate saucepan heat chicken with butter, add 2 tablespoons of sauce and sherry wine. Add yolk of egg to remaining sauce with grated cheese. Make omelet and fold in chicken, place in baking dish, cover with sauce, sprinkle with grated cheese. Bake in very hot oven until golden brown.

Henri Soulé, Le Pavillon Restaurant, New York City

Crabmeat à la Newburg

2 cups crabmeat	1 tbsp. flour
4 tbsps. butter	1 cup cream
½ tsp. paprika	2 egg yolks (beaten)
⅓ cup sherry	Salt and pepper

Heat but do not brown the crabmeat together with 3 tablespoons of the butter, the sherry, and paprika. While crabmeat is heating melt the remaining tablespoon of butter and blend with the flour in the top of a double boiler. Add the cream and stir constantly till hot. Pour slowly 2 tablespoon of this hot cream sauce into the beaten egg yolks; continue to beat them until the cream is thoroughly mixed into the yolks. Then pour this mixture into the double boiler and stir in the remaining sauce. Continue stirring about 2 minutes until sauce is smooth and thickens. Add crabmeat, salt, and pepper to taste, stir and serve on toast. Serves 4.

Emily Post, New York City

Virginia Sunday Night Casserole

2 tbsps. butter		2 cups (equal parts)
2 tbsps. flour	make	ground cooked ham,
2 cups milk	medium	tongue, chicken
Salt and paprika	white sauce	

Mix together.

Have casserole well buttered. Put in layer of mixture, cover with chopped hard-boiled eggs, bread crumbs, and dot with butter. Repeat. Cover with more chopped egg, breadcrumbs, and butter. Bake in moderate oven until brown.

Miss Charlotte Noland, Foxcroft School, Virginia

Spanish Roast Chicken

Roasting chicken	Anchovy fillets
Thin slices of oranges and lemons	Strips of bacon
Stuffed olives	Red wine

Cover the bottom of a roasting pan with thin slices of orange, on top of each round of orange place a slice of lemon. Sprinkle about a dozen stuffed olives and several anchovy fillets over the fruit. Rub the chicken inside and out with lemon juice, set it (without stuffing) on the prepared bed and cover the breast and legs with strips of bacon to keep them from getting too well done in the beginning. Put in the oven, about 375 degrees, and roast in the usual way but keep basting with red wine (you use about ½ bottle of red wine per chicken). As the fruit melts down, scoop the syrup up from the bottom of the pan and baste with it as well as with the wine. You can take some of the grease off the gravy before serving if you wish. This dish can be prepared in advance and kept warm till served.

Ilka Chase, New York City

Neptune Nonsense

½ lb. scallops	4 hard-boiled eggs
½ green pepper, cut fine	¼ tsp. onion juice
1 tbsp. mayonnaise	½ tsp. Worcestershire sauce
1 envelope gelatine	¼ tsp. dry mustard
1 tsp. salt	4 tsps. lemon juice
Pepper	A dash of chili sauce
½ lb. cooked shrimps	

Cook scallops 10 minutes with 2 cups salted water. Cool. Grind shrimps, scallops, eggs, and green peppers together. Add 1 cup liquid from scallops. Soften gelatine in ¼ cup cold liquid from scallops and dissolve in remaining liquid heated. Mix all these ingredients and put in a mold to jell. Turn it out onto a platter. Serve with whole shrimps as decoration, sliced tomatoes, and "New Orleans" sauce.

New Orleans Sauce

1 cup mayonnaise	½ tsp. chili powder
½ cup chili sauce	½ tsp. salt
2 tsps. lemon juice	½ tsp. prepared mustard
3 tsps. horseradish	¼ tsp. pepper

Mix together.

Salvador Dalí, New York City

Soufflé Surprise

2 tbsps. orange marmalade	4 egg whites beaten stiff
3 tbsps. sugar	Shredded almonds (optional)
¼ cup orange juice	Whipped cream, sweetened and
¼ cup orange liqueur (Cointreau,	liqueur-flavored, for sauce
Curaçao or Grand Marnier)	

Mix together marmalade, sugar, orange juice, and liqueur. Fold into this, lightly but thoroughly, beaten egg whites. Pour mixture into well buttered top of 2-quart double boiler, set over hot water on moderate fire. Cook, uncovered, 40 minutes without disturbing. Turn onto a platter, sprinkle with almonds; serve with flavored whipped cream. Note: You can use other combinations of liqueurs or jams, too—as for instance, tangerine marmalade with peach brandy; damson preserve with Kümmel, etc. Serves 4.

Mrs. Harold E. Talbott, New York City

Duck with Cherries

1 4-lb. duck	1 cup red wine
2 tbsps. brandy	½ cup stock
2 tbsps. butter	1-lb. can black cherries
1 tsp. B.V. meat glaze	2 tbsps. sherry
2 tsps. potato flour	¾ cup cherry juice
1 tbsp. red currant jelly	Salt and pepper

Cut duck up as for casserole and brown very quickly, starting skin side first, in the hot butter. Heat brandy, light, and pour over duck. Remove duck from pan. Stir into pan, off the fire, the meat glaze, potato flour. When smooth, pour on the cherry juice, stock, red wine, currant jelly, and sherry. Add salt, pepper and stir over the fire until boiling. Then add the pitted cherries and put back the duck. Cover with wax paper and the lid, and cook slowly for 40–50 minutes. Serve in a casserole.

Mrs. Dione Lucas, Cordon Bleu Cooking School, New York City

Beef "à la Créole"

1 3-lb. pot roast	½ cup oil
2 onions	¼ cup vinegar
Garlic	1 small can tomato paste
Thyme	Butter
Laurel leaves	White bread
Parsley	Salt and pepper

Cut pot roast in slices. Put them in deep dish with salt, pepper, 2 sliced onions, little garlic, thyme, 3 or 4 laurel leaves, parsley, oil, and vinegar. Leave for 12 hours, then put the whole thing in pan and let cook on a slow fire for 2½ hours. Add tomato paste and let cook for ½ hour more. Remove meat from pan and keep it warm. Let sauce reduce and strain it thoroughly. Brown in butter slices of white bread. Put meat in center of a dish, dispose browned bread around, pour sauce over.

Mrs. Blanche Knopf, New York City

Creamed Calf's Liver

The liver must not touch the ice. Skin liver, then slice about ½ an inch thick. Partly fry in butter and season with salt and pepper. Trim slices, making square pieces, and place trimmings with a pinch of flour in a frying pan. After cooking add half-and-half cream and milk to make a soft consistency; pass through a very fine sieve. Heat in a double boiler, then add remaining liver. Place in a cream sauce a few minutes before serving. Season to taste.

Mrs. Ector Munn, New York City

Rognon de Veau Grillé aux Champignons Frais
(Veal Kidney Broiled with Mushrooms)

1 veal kidney	1 tsp. fresh chopped parsley
½ lb. mushrooms	3 tbsps. sweet butter
Juice of ½ lemon	

To cook, split the veal kidney through its widest part. Trim the fat, leaving just enough to cover the kidney. Season with salt and pepper, coat with melted butter, place inside of a wire rack, and set to broil briskly. When browned on both sides, remove the kidney to a sauté pan, and finish the cooking in a hot oven for 2 to 3 minutes.

To serve: Separate the kidney in two, place on a hot serving dish, add the butter, the lemon juice, and chopped parsley in the sauté pan while stirring. Correct the seasoning and pour over the kidney.

You have meanwhile peeled and fried the mushrooms, season well. Serve these with a bouquet of watercress on the same plate. Serves 2.

Joseph Donon, chef for Mrs. Hamilton McKnown Twombly, New York City

Rognons d'Agneau Sautés Chasseur
(Lamb Kidneys Chasseur)

5 lamb kidneys	½ cup dry white wine
1 level tsp. flour	½ cup stock or water
1 shallot, very finely chopped	1 tsp. coarsely chopped parsley
½ lb. mushrooms	Salt and pepper
2 tbsps. Madeira wine	

Remove the outer skin from lamb kidneys, split them in two, then each half into 4 slices. Season with salt and pepper and fry briskly in clarified butter. Then drain this cooking butter, sprinkle the shallot over the kidneys, toss for an instant over the fire, add the flour, toss a little more and pour in the Madeira and white wine, and if too thick, add a little stock or more wine or water. Bring to a boil, add the mushrooms which have been peeled, sliced, and fried briskly in clarified butter. Season to taste, simmer for 2 to 3 minutes, and serve with parsley sprinkled over the top. Note: Serve in copper dish or in casserole with wild rice. Serves 2.

Joseph Donon, chef for Mrs. Hamilton McKnown Twombly, New York City

Veal Chops en Papillote

Veal chops	Parsley, shallots (2 for 6 chops)
Flour, butter, salt, pepper	Tarragon (optional)
Waxed paper, cooking oil	Bread crumbs

It is important to get good veal chops. Dip them lightly in flour. Sauté them in a pan containing very hot butter, add salt and pepper. Brown the chops well on both sides, but see that the butter does not burn. Do not put a cover on the pan. Cook until almost done. The next step is to get some pieces of paper ready for the chops, using a piece of waxed paper large enough to contain 1 chop. Leave enough length at the ends to be able to twist the paper tightly. Brush each piece of paper lightly with oil, using a brush for this purpose. Chop finely and sauté parsley, shallots, and tarragon if you have it. Place the chop in the center of the paper, but before you do this scatter some bread crumbs and small pieces of butter on the paper. One tablespoonful chopped herbs for 1 chop. Now place the chop on top of this. Sprinkle the top of the chop with the sautéed herbs and a tiny bit more bread crumbs, dotting with several small pieces of butter. Wrap it and twist the ends of the paper. Cook in a medium oven so the paper will not burn, for about 25 minutes. Serve in the papers.

Marquise Galcerand de Pins, Beaulieu Vineyard, Rutherford, California

Poached Peaches à la Virgil Thomson

12 ripe peaches or nectarines	1 box fresh or frozen raspberries
1 cup sugar	Liqueur glass of kirsch (optional)

Plunge peaches or nectarines, skins on, in boiling water. Leave till just cooked when tested with a fork, which should take only 2 to 3 minutes. Remove and peel. Leave the peaches to cool in a colander, catching whatever juice drips from them. Save the peelings. Make a syrup in the poaching water with sugar, peelings, and raspberries. Strain the syrup through a fine sieve, add the drippings from the peaches and reduce it to a consistency not too thick. Cool and pour over the peaches. Serve lukewarm or at room temperature. Do not chill. Add kirsch to the syrup before pouring it over the peaches (makes the dessert even more delectable). Use the best peaches, preferably white clingstones.

Virgil Thomson, New York City

Gigot à la Périgord

(a French XVIII century recipe)

Leg of mutton	Chives, parsley, garlic
Truffles, French bacon or	Thin sheets of veal and
fresh salt pork	fresh salt pork
Spices, salt, herbs (as marjoram,	
sage, or oregano)	

Take a leg of mutton, truffles, and French bacon (not smoked, just fresh pork). Cut truffles and bacon in tiny bits; stir them with salt and spices, chopped parsley, chives, and a point of garlic. Then lard all over the leg of mutton with these truffles and bacon. Wrap it very carefully in wax paper and leave it for several hours—not in icebox. Tie on a blanketing of thin slices of veal and strips of fresh salt pork. Cook it very slowly without further addition, and serve the leg of mutton with its own gravy.

Editorial Note: This recipe is delectable. For an 8-pound leg of lamb, use 5 truffles (4 for larding, 1 cut up in gravy), about ⅛ pound fresh salt pork for larding, and extra sheets of same for blanketing (the amount you would need to wrap a pheasant is sufficient). Have veal cutlet, bone removed, sliced lengthwise in 4 or 5 thin sheets for blanketing. Tie securely with cord. Roast slowly in oven for 2¾ hours. De-grease gravy before serving, remove cord, but not blanketing. Serves 10.

Christian Dior

About the Contributors

Select Biographies

Elizabeth Arden was an entrepreneur who created the first North American cosmetics empire. She introduced the "Total Look," the concept of utilizing matching or coordinated lip, cheek, and nail color. By 1915, she had expanded her business worldwide. The Elizabeth Arden brand was considered one of the world's most upscale cosmetic companies, counting celebrities and royals such as Marlene Dietrich, Joan Crawford, and the Duchess of Windsor as clients.

Mrs. Vincent Astor, née Helen Dinsmore Huntington, married Vincent Astor, the son of millionaire John Jacob Astor IV, in 1913. At the outbreak of World War I, when her husband joined the Navy on the advice of his friend Franklin D. Roosevelt (see **Roosevelt**), she joined him overseas, performing charity work with the YMCA in France. The couple divorced in 1940.

George Baker, a commercial artist and draughtsman hired by Walt Disney in 1937, assisted in the production of many full-length Disney features, among them *Pinocchio* (1940), *Fantasia* (1940), and *Bambi* (1942). Drafted into the army in 1941, he was soon hired by *Yank, the Army Magazine*, where his cartoons about the travails of an army recruit, *The Sad Sack*, became the publication's most popular feature and later a syndicated comic strip and comic book series.

Tallulah Bankhead was a stage and film actress known for her wit, outlandish behavior, and hard-partying, promiscuous ways. She starred on Broadway, most notably in Lillian Hellman's *The Three Little Foxes* (1939–40), Thornton Wilder's *The Skin of Our Teeth* (1942–43), and a 1949 revival of *Private Lives* by Noël Coward (see **Coward**). Married to actor John Emery (1937–1941), she was linked romantically to Chico Marx, Gary Cooper, Greta Garbo, and Marlene Dietrich, among others.

Philip Barry was a playwright best known for *The Philadelphia Story* (1939). The Broadway production became a hit starring Katharine Hepburn (see **Hepburn**). She bought the movie rights and starred in the 1940 film version directed by George Cukor, who also adapted Barry's 1928 play, *Holiday*, for the screen.

Cecil Beaton was an acerbically witty fashion and portrait photographer whose work appeared in *Vogue* and *Vanity Fair* for five decades. He often photographed Hollywood celebrities and society figures, including England's royal family. After World War II, he designed sets, costumes, and lighting for Broadway shows and film musicals, earning Academy Awards for Costume Design for his work on *Gigi* (1958) and *My Fair Lady* (1964).

Lucius Beebe, a gourmand and author of more than thirty books, has been credited with popularizing the term "café society." Expelled from both Yale and Harvard for bad behavior (one prank involved chartering an airplane to cover J. P. Morgan's yacht in toilet paper), Beebe found his way into journalism, chronicling high-society life in "This New York," his syndicated column (1930–1944) for the *New York Herald Tribune*. He also wrote about restaurants around the world, notably in "Along the Boulevard," a column for *Gourmet* magazine.

Lucrezia Bori was a soprano at New York's Metropolitan Opera (1910–1936). Best known for her portrayals of Mimi in Puccini's *La Bohème*, Mélisande in Debussy's *Pelléas et Mélisande*, and Manon in the Massenet opera of the same name, she was a beloved performer. Upon her retirement, she was elected to the company's board of directors and became chairman of the Metropolitan Opera Guild.

Mrs. Charles Boyer, née Pat Paterson, was an actress who wed French actor Charles Boyer in 1934. The couple was married for forty-four years. When Pat died in 1978, Charles Boyer committed suicide two days later. Charles Boyer frequently played a sophisticated ladies' man in both European and American movies. He appeared in more than eighty films, receiving four Academy Award nominations for Best Actor for *Conquest* (1937), opposite Greta Garbo; *Algiers*, the 1938 remake of the classic French movie *Pépé le Moko*; *Gaslight* (1944), with Ingrid Bergman; and *Fanny* (1961), with Leslie Caron and Maurice Chevalier.

Fanny Brice was a former Ziegfeld Follies headliner and a comedienne best remembered for creating "Baby Snooks," a widely popular bratty toddler she portrayed on CBS and NBC radio programs from the 1930s until her death in 1951. Barbra Streisand won an Academy Award for Best Actress for her portrayal of Brice in *Funny Girl* (1968).

Louis Bromfield, best-selling author of more than thirty fiction and nonfiction books, won the Pulitzer Prize for Fiction in 1926 for his second novel, *Early Autumn*. A Francophile decorated for his work with the American Field Service during World War I, he later spent a decade living in France. Upon his return to the United States in the late 1930s, he became known as a visionary conservationist who developed principles of sustainable farming at Malabar, his farm in Ohio.

Pearl S. Buck, winner of the 1932 Pulitzer Prize for Fiction for her novel *The Good Earth*, was the first American woman to be awarded the Nobel Prize for Literature (1938). She spent her childhood and a large part of her adult life in China, first with her Presbyterian missionary parents, then with her husband, an agricultural economist. Her concern about poverty and discrimination prompted her to establish Welcome House, the first international interracial adoption agency, in 1949.

Charlie Chaplin was an actor, director, and composer best known for portraying a vagrant with refined manners in silent-era films such as *The Kid* (1921) and *The Pilgrim* (1923). After co-founding the first independent film production company, United Artists, with Mary Pickford (see **Pickford**) and others in 1919, he made *City Lights* (1931) and *Modern Times* (1936). He came to the talkies late with *The Great Dictator* (1940), *Monsieur Verdoux* (1947), and *Limelight* (1952). Nominated for an Academy Award on several occasions, he won an Oscar for Best Original Music Score for *Limelight*, as well as two Honorary Academy Awards.

Ilka Chase was the daughter of Edna Woolman Chase, the editor of *Vogue* magazine (1914–1952). She appeared in films such as *Fast and Loose* (1930) and *Now, Voyager* (1942; see **Cooper**). Chase was the first to portray Sally Fowler on stage in *The Women* (1938) by Clare Boothe Luce (see **Luce**). She hosted a number of radio shows, including the gossip- and advice-filled *Luncheon at the Waldorf.* She later served as a panelist on television's *Celebrity Time, Masquerade Party,* and *Keep Talking.*

Constance Collier was an actress who appeared in films such as *Stage Door* (1937), along with Katharine Hepburn (see **Hepburn**), with whom she became fast friends; *Kitty* (1945); Alfred Hitchcock's *Rope* (1948); and Otto Preminger's *Whirlpool* (1949).

Gladys Cooper began her acting career on the stage but ultimately had success in Hollywood, where she was most frequently cast as an aristocrat. Her portrayals of Bette Davis's domineering mother in *Now, Voyager* (1942; see **Chase**), a nun in *Song of Bernadette* (1943), and Rex Harrison's mother in *My Fair Lady* (1964; see **Beaton**) earned her three Academy Award nominations for Best Supporting Actress.

Katharine Cornell was a stage actress, writer, and producer noted for major roles in Broadway dramas. Like her friend Helen Hayes (see **Hayes**), she was nicknamed the "First Lady of the Theater." A tragedienne, she famously portrayed poet Elizabeth Barrett Browning in the 1931 Broadway production of *The Barretts of Wimpole Street.*

Noël Coward wrote more than fifty plays and a number of popular songs during a six-decade career. Renowned for his wit, personal style, and taste for the high life, Coward embodied glamour between the two world wars, during which he produced his most enduring hits: *Hay Fever* (1925), *Private Lives* (1930), *Design for Living* (1933), *Present Laughter* (1939), and *Blithe Spirit* (1941).

Mrs. Drexel Dahlgren, née Lucy Wharton Drexel, was the daughter of Drexel, Morgan and Co. founder and philanthropist Joseph W. Drexel. She married Eric Dahlgren, a son of Admiral John A. Dahlgren (inventor of the Civil War-era Dhalgren gun), in 1890 and divorced him in 1912. In 1915, she hired architect and interior designer Ogden Codman Jr. (Edith Wharton's collaborator on the classic book, *The Decoration of Houses*, 1887) to design her townhouse on 96th Street and Fifth Avenue, which she later leased to jeweler Pierre Cartier.

Salvador Dalí was an artist known for his surrealist art, particularly *The Persistence of Memory* (1931), which features liquified watches draped over a barren landscape. Known for his flamboyant behavior and personal style, Dalí also worked in film, with Luis Buñuel on *Un Chien Andalou* (1929) and *L'Age d'Or* (1930), and with Alfred Hitchcock on the dream sequence for *Spellbound* (1945). He collaborated with Elsa Schiaparelli (see **Schiaparelli**) on a lobster-print dress, a shoe-shaped hat, and a lip-buckle belt.

Duc de Verdura, formally known as Fulco Santostefano della Cerda, Duc de Verdura, was born to an aristocratic Italian family whose financial ruin led him to seek refuge in Paris 1926. There,

Cole Porter (see **Porter**) helped him find work with Coco Chanel, for whom Verdura eventually designed the multicolored Malta crosses and chains that have remained the couture house's trademarks. Moving to New York just before World War II, Verdura went on to design jewels for Katharine Hepburn (see **Hepburn**), cigarette cases for Porter, as well as extravagant bracelets, necklaces, hat pins, and brooches featured regularly in *Harper's Bazaar* and *Vogue*.

Christian Dior was a French couturier whose first collection in February 1947 marked the rebirth of haute couture and the return of Paris as its center. Called the "New Look," the landmark collection emphasized the curves of the female form and made Dior an instant sensation, especially among Hollywood celebrities and New York socialites. Soon thereafter identified with good taste and the refined culture that epitomized Paris to the rest of the world, Dior capitalized on this interest by opening a fur subsidiary and a ready-to-wear boutique on New York City's Fifth Avenue.

Countess di Zoppola, née Edith Mortimer, was known to her friends as Tookie. A prominent New York society figure, she often held house parties at her estate near Oyster Bay, Long Island. She was riding with the Duc de Verdura (see **de Verdura**) and Cole Porter in the fall of 1937 when the composer had his terrible, life-altering accident (see **Porter**).

Mrs. Angier Biddle Duke, née Priscilla St. George, married Angier Biddle Duke, an American Tobacco Company heir and Yale dropout, in 1937. After a round-the-world honeymoon, the couple settled in New York's Tuxedo Park, with Angier working as an editor in Manhattan. He became well known for his excesses, including fast driving while intoxicated, and the couple divorced in 1940. Angier Biddle Duke went on to serve as ambassador to El Salvador, Denmark, Spain, and Morocco, and as chief of protocol for Presidents Kennedy and Johnson.

Lynn Fontanne was celebrated for her roles in high comedy and elegant romantic plays and movies. Married to Alfred Lunt (see **Lunt**), she was part of one the most famous acting couples in United States history. From the 1920s onward, she acted almost exclusively with her husband, appearing with him in numerous productions including Shakespeare's *The Taming of the Shrew* (1935–36) and Robert E. Sherwood's *There Shall Be No Light* (1940). She received an Academy Award nomination for Best Actress in *The Guardsman* (1931) but lost to lifelong friend Helen Hayes (see **Hayes**).

Mrs. Samuel Goldwyn, née Frances Howard, was an American actress who made four films between 1925 and 1935. She is best known as the second and last wife of Academy Award–winning producer Samuel Goldwyn.

Helen Hayes's seventy-year career on stage earned her the title of "First Lady of American Theater." She starred in Booth Tarkington's 1920 *Clarence* with Alfred Lunt (see **Lunt**), reportedly falling in love with him just as he met his future wife, Lynn Fontanne (see **Fontanne**). Hayes launched her Hollywood career with *The Sin of Madelon Claudet* (1931), for which she won the Academy Award for Best Actress. She also starred in *A Farewell* *to Arms* (1932), *Anastasia* (1956), and *Airport* (1971), the latter for which she won her second Academy Award. She was presented with the National Medal of Arts in 1988.

Mrs. William Randolph Hearst, née Millicent Wilson, was a sixteen-year-old "bicycle girl" at the Herald Square Theater in 1897 when she met thirty-four-year-old William Randolph Hearst, who was then on the verge of becoming the greatest newspaper baron in the United States. Married in 1903, the couple had five sons together but divorced in 1926. From then on, Mrs. Hearst established herself in New York City's political and social circles through her charitable activities, most notably the Free Milk Fund for Babies, which she founded in 1921.

Katharine Hepburn was a film, stage, and television actress who won a record four Academy Awards for Best Actress, out of twelve nominations, for her performances in *Morning Glory* (1933), *Guess Who's Coming to Dinner?* (1967), *The Lion in Winter* (1968), and *On Golden Pond* (1981). Renowned for her athleticism, mental agility, polished style, and clipped New England accent, she starred in many classic films, including *Bringing Up Baby* (1938), *The Philadelphia Story* (1940; see **Barry**), *The African Queen* (1951), and *Long Day's Journey Into Night* (1962).

Aldous Huxley was renowned for his thought-provoking writing and pessimistic views about the future of society, as exemplified in his works *Point Counterpoint* (1928), *Brave New World* (1932), and *Eyeless in Gaza* (1936). In 1937 Huxley moved to Hollywood, where he worked as a screenwriter for *Pride and Prejudice* (1940), *Madame Curie* (1943), and *Jane Eyre* (1944).

A pioneer of psychedelic drug use, he wrote about his experiences in *The Doors of Perception* (1954), from which the rock 'n' roll band The Doors took its name.

Helen Keller was an author, activist, and lecturer whose globe-trotting advocacy for the blind earned her a Presidential Medal of Freedom in 1964 and an election to the National Women's Hall of Fame in 1965. Deaf and blind as a result of an early childhood illness, Keller broke through her near-complete isolation with the help of instructor Anne Sullivan, eventually gaining admission to Radcliffe College. Upon graduating in 1904, she became the first deaf-and-blind person to earn a bachelor's degree. A well-traveled intellectual and a prolific author, she campaigned for women's suffrage, workers' rights, and socialism, and was outspoken in her opposition to war.

Blanche Knopf worked with her husband, Alfred A. Knopf, to establish in 1915 the New York publishing house still known by his name today. She is credited for bringing the works of Sigmund Freud, Albert Camus, André Gide, Jean-Paul Sartre, Simone de Beauvoir, and Thomas Mann to the United States.

Vivien Leigh was a stage and film actress best known for portraying Scarlett O'Hara in *Gone with the Wind* (1939) and Blanche DuBois in the film version of *A Streetcar Named Desire* (1951). She won Academy Awards for Best Actress for each performance. During her thirty-year career, Leigh took on a variety of stage roles, many of these performed with husband Laurence Olivier (see **Olivier**).

Anita Loos was a screenwriter, playwright, and author. She is best known for *Gentlemen Prefer Blondes*, short sketches first published in *Harper's Bazaar*, then in book form in 1925. She wrote the scripts for *Red-Headed Woman* (1932), starring Jean Harlow, and *Gigi* (1958), starring Leslie Caron. She adapted *The Women* by Clare Boothe Luce (see **Luce**) for film and wrote regularly for *Vanity Fair* and *The New Yorker*.

Clare Boothe Luce was first known as an editor and journalist for *Vogue* and *Vanity Fair*. After marrying publisher Henry Luce in 1935, she focused on her career as a playwright (*Abide with Me*, 1935; *The Women*, 1936; *Kiss the Boys Goodbye*, 1938) and eventually became a journalist for *Time*. She collected her wartime observations in *Europe in the Spring* (1940). Luce was one of the first women to be elected to the House of Representatives, serving two terms as a Republican (1942–1947). She campaigned on behalf of Dwight D. Eisenhower during his presidential run, after which he appointed her ambassador to Italy. She was awarded the Presidential Medal of Freedom in 1983.

Alfred Lunt was a stage actor and director celebrated for his comic skills and impeccable timing, particularly when performing with his wife Lynn Fontanne (see **Fontanne**), whom he married in 1922. The pair enjoyed tremendous success acting together in more than twenty plays, including *Design for Living* (1933) by Noël Coward (see **Coward**). Lunt received an Academy Award Nomination for Best Actor in *The Guardsman* (1931).

Mrs. Charles H. Marshall, née Roberta Brooke Russell, is better known today as Brooke Astor, the former chairwoman of the Vincent Astor Foundation. Vincent Astor, her third husband, was a son of multimillionaire John Jacob Astor IV, who inherited his fortune when his father died aboard the *Titanic* in 1912. She and Astor married in 1953. He established the foundation at that time, leaving it to her to run upon his death in 1959. Prior to Astor, Brooke was married to Charles H. Marshall from 1932 until his death in 1952. Marshall was a senior partner in an investment firm and a brother-in-law of mercantile heir Marshall Field II.

Curtis Moffat was a photographer of abstract pictures, color still lifes, and society portraits. In the 1920s he studied photography in New York and in Paris, where he collaborated with Man Ray. He later moved to London, where he met some of the most important figures of twentieth-century cultural life, notably Cecil Beaton (see **Beaton**), who later credited Moffat with influencing his work. Moffat was also a pivotal figure in modernist interior design.

Condé Nast was one of the world's most successful magazine publishers. After spending a decade at *Collier's*, Nast bought *Vogue*, then a small New York society magazine, in 1909, and soon transformed it into a premier fashion publication. After buying interests in *House & Garden* and *Travel* in 1911, Nast added *Dress* and *Vanity Fair* to his roster in 1913, turning the latter into a sophisticated general-interest magazine. Although the Great Depression had a ruinous effect on his business, in 1939 Nast launched *Glamour*, whose highly innovative use of a "crowded" layout and recognition of Hollywood's influence on fashion and beauty trends in society made it an instant success.

Prince Serge Obolensky fought with the anti-Bolshevik Tartars during the Bolshevik Revolution. Forced into hiding in Moscow, he escaped to England, where he served as a soldier in World War I. There he met Ava Alice Muriel Astor, daughter of Colonel John Jacob Astor IV and sister to Vincent Astor (see **Marshall**), who had moved to London with her mother after her parents divorced. The couple was married in 1924—after Obolensky divorced Catherine Alexandrovna Romanov, daughter of Czar Alexander II—and moved to New York. There he became a hotel-business legend, overseeing the operations of many grand hotels, including the Plaza, Sherry Netherland, St. Regis, Ambassador, and Astor.

Laurence Olivier's remarkable six-decade acting career included a wide variety of stage, film, and television roles. Among many other distinctions, he earned fourteen Academy Award nominations, with two wins for Best Actor and Best Picture for *Hamlet* (1948), which he directed. As one of the twentieth century's top interpreters of Shakespeare, he sat on the board of directors of London's Old Vic and became the inaugural director of the National Theater of England. While filming *Fire Over England* (1937), in which he was cast opposite Vivien Leigh, Olivier began an affair with his costar (see **Leigh**), marrying her in 1940.

Mrs. Paul Pennoyer was the wife of Paul Geddes Pennoyer, a Harvard-trained lawyer who worked for the New York firm White & Case, which provided legal services to many of the companies financed by J. P. Morgan. After working for the Pentagon during World War II, Paul Pennoyer served as secretary for a commission of the 1946 U.N. Conference on International Organization in San Francisco. Mrs. Paul G. Pennoyer came to J. P. Morgan's side in the tiny Florida Keys village where he died following a heart attack in 1953.

Mary Pickford achieved her acting fame in nickelodeon pictures. Known as "America's sweetheart" from her portrayals of barefoot adolescents and urchins in features such as *Hearts Adrift* and *Tess of the Storm Country*, she was a pioneer of the cinema. In 1919, she co-founded the first independent film production company, United Artists, with D. W. Griffith, Charlie Chaplin (see **Chaplin**), and Douglas Fairbanks, whom she married the following year. Dinners at the Pickford-Fairbanks mansion in Beverly Hills were legendary, with an impressive list of guests that included George Bernard Shaw, Amelia Earhart, Albert Einstein, F. Scott Fitzgerald, and Noël Coward (see **Coward**), among others.

Lily Pons was a principal soprano at the New York Metropolitan Opera from 1931 to 1960. Discovered by an impresario as she sang in French provincial opera houses, Pons auditioned for the Met when the opera house was seeking to replace star coloratura Amelita Galli-Curci upon her 1930 retirement. Pons became a sensation upon her January 1931 debut, portraying Lucia in Donizetti's *Lucia di Lammermoor*.

Mrs. Cole Porter, née Linda Belle Lee Thomas, met musical theater composer Cole Porter at the wedding of railroad heiress Ethel Harriman and Henry Potter Russell at the Ritz in Paris in 1918. Divorced from *New York Morning Telegraph* owner Edward R. Thomas, she had led a life of luxury and leisure during her first marriage, a lifestyle that continued into her thirty-four-year marriage to Porter. Mrs. Porter entertained lavishly at the couple's homes in Paris and New York, and she accommodated the composer's homosexual relationships. She cared for her husband with devotion following his 1937 riding accident, when his horse reared, fell, rolled on him, and broke both his legs (see **di Zoppola**). As a result, Porter endured thirty operations and was in chronic pain and largely crippled for the rest of his life.

Emily Post, née Emily Price, was born into privilege as the only daughter of a Baltimore architect. After divorcing her husband Edwin Post in 1905, she turned to writing newspaper articles on architecture and interior design, as well as light novels. Her 1922 book, *Etiquette in Society, in Business, in Politics and at Home*, was a bestseller. Almost a hundred years later, the Post book and name are still synonymous with proper etiquette and manners.

Mrs. Laurance Rockefeller, née Mary Montague French, was the granddaughter of nineteenth-century Northern Pacific Rail-road president Frederick Billings. A childhood friendship with Laurance Rockefeller led to marriage in 1934. She was a dedicated supporter of the YWCA, holding various executive positions in the organization's international divisions. Her husband, a successful venture capitalist, financier, and conservationist, was the fourth of John D. Rockefeller Jr. and Abby Aldrich Rockefeller's six children and a grandson of Standard Oil Company founder John D. Rockefeller.

Mrs. Franklin Delano Roosevelt, née Anna Eleanor Roosevelt (her father was Franklin Delano Roosevelt's fifth cousin), was the First Lady of the United States from 1933 to 1945. She transformed the role of first lady by traveling throughout the United States and the world, expressing her opinions candidly in the media, including her own syndicated newspaper column. She fought for the status of women in the workforce, African-American civil rights, and human rights worldwide. She chaired the committee that drafted and approved the 1948 *Universal Declaration of Human Rights*. President Harry Truman called her the "First Lady of the World" in recognition of her human rights achievements.

Mrs. James Roosevelt, née Sara Ann Delano, doted on her only child, Franklin Delano Roosevelt. A distant cousin of Eleanor Roosevelt, she knew Eleanor (see **Mrs. Franklin Delano Roosevelt**) long before Franklin fell in love with her. Believing Eleanor to be unprepared for her role in a prominent family, Sara fiercely resisted her son's desire to marry Eleanor, ultimately becoming a dominant presence in the relationship after the wedding in 1905. Nevertheless, she helped save her son's marriage when his liaison with Eleanor's personal secretary, Lucy Mercer, was discovered in 1918: Sara argued that divorce would bring scandal to the family and that she would disinherit Franklin if he went through with it.

Princess Kyril Scherbatow, née Adelaide Sedgwick Munroe, married Russian aristocrat Prince Scherbatow in 1939. Together they operated guest homes for society and celebrity visitors in Jamaica and Bermuda. She died in 1968. Prince Scherbatow fled Russia after the Bolshevik Revolution, working in various professions in Turkey, Bulgaria, and Belgium. He turned to banking in Brussels and Paris in the 1920s and immigrated to the United States in 1932 as a representative for Veuve Cliquot champagne.

Gogo Schiaparelli, formally known as Countess Maria Luisa Yvonne Radha de Wendt de Kerlor, was the daughter of Franco-Swiss theosophist Count William de Wendt de Kerlor and Italian-born, Paris and New York–based fashion designer Elsa Schiaparelli. In 1941, Gogo married Robert Lawrence Berenson, vice president of the Grace Line shipping fleet and second cousin to illustrious expatriate art critic and advisor Bernard Berenson. The couple had two daughters, model-actress Marisa Berenson and photographer Berry Berenson, who was married to actor Anthony Perkins.

Norma Shearer was one of the world's most popular actresses during her heyday in the 1920s and 1930s. MGM's box-office darling was also a pioneer in feminism, as she made it acceptable—even chic—to portray an unmarried, sexual woman on screen. She married MGM executive Irving Thalberg in 1927, the year she completed her most famous silent movie, Ernst Lubitsch's *The Student Prince in Old Heidelberg*. Nominated for an Academy Award for Best Actress on six occasions, she won for her role in *The Divorcee* (1930), a talkie.

William Rhinelander Stewart was a descendant of one of New York's oldest and most prominent families. A major fixture on the Manhattan nightclub scene in the 1930s, he was often photographed while out on the town with Cole Porter (see **Porter**). A true bon vivant, Stewart was said never to get up before noon. His wife, Janet, was known as the most beautiful woman in New York and was included in the first International Best-Dressed List in 1940.

Mrs. Igor Stravinsky, née Vera de Bosset, had been the maestro's lover for nearly two decades when she married him in March 1940 after the death of his first wife. Mr. Stravinsky, one of the most influential composers of the twentieth century, gained international recognition with *The Firebird* (1910), *Petrushka* (1911), and *The Rite of Spring* (1913), commissioned by Serge Diaghilev for his Ballets Russes in Paris. Born in Russia, Stravinsky moved to the United States at the outbreak of World War II, settling in West Hollywood. He became part of Los Angeles's growing cultural life, forming friendships with musicians, composers, and writers there, notably Aldous Huxley (see **Huxley**).

Deems Taylor was a composer, music critic, and promoter of classical music. After creating well-received works for orchestra and voice, he became the music critic for the *New York World* in 1921 and composed two new operas for the Metropolitan Opera, *The King's Henchman* (1927) and *Peter Ibbertson* (1929). A broadcaster and commentator for the New York Philharmonic, he served as master of ceremonies in Disney's 1940 film, *Fantasia*, for which he selected musical pieces.

Virgil Thomson was a composer and critic who played a central role in the development of the "American Sound" in classical music. Following his 1939 book *The State of Music*, Thomson established himself as a composer and as music critic for the *New York Herald Tribune* (1940–1951). He created pieces rooted in American speech rhythms and hymnbook harmony and is best known for the operas *Four Saints in Three Acts* (1927–1928) and *The Mother of Us All* (1946–1947), both with texts by Gertrude Stein.

Lawrence Tibbett was one of the most successful American baritones at the New York Metropolitan Opera (1923–1950). He is best known for his portrayals of Iago in Verdi's *Otello*, Scarpia in Puccini's *Tosca*, and Escamillo in Bizet's *Carmen*. A recording artist and actor, he performed both Porgy and Jake in the first album of selections from George Gershwin's *Porgy and Bess*. He also had a Packard Motor Car Company–sponsored radio program in the 1930s, on which he sang formal music—and announced the 1935 Packard One-Twenty to the world—on air.

Mrs. Hamilton McKnown Twombly, née Florence Vanderbilt, was the sixth-born child of William H. Vanderbilt and Maria Kissam Vanderbilt and granddaughter of Commodore Cornelius Vanderbilt. Florence was twenty-three when her grandfather died in 1877, leaving her with an inheritance worth more than $100 million. She married railroad tycoon Hamilton Twombly that same year and became the apotheosis of New York society for the next seventy-five years. In addition to her mansions on Fifth Avenue and in Newport, Rhode Island, she was mistress of Horham in Madison, New Jersey, a 1,000-acre estate with a Georgian-style house designed by architects McKim, Meade & White, with more than one hundred rooms and an indoor swimming pool. To the end of her life, Mrs. Twombly employed a staff of about one hundred, a third of them gardeners.

Valentina, née Valentina Nicholaevna Sanina, was a Russian-born fashion and theatrical costume designer. After marrying financier George Schlee in 1928, she opened a small couture dress house, Valentina's Gowns, on Madison Avenue. She dressed prominent New York society women as well as actresses such as Lynn Fontanne (see **Fontanne**), Gloria Swanson, Katharine Hepburn (see **Hepburn**), and Greta Garbo. In 1941, Garbo began a two-decade affair with Schlee. Because they lived in the same building, the two women set up an elaborate schedule to avoid each other in the lobby.

Mrs. William H. Vanderbilt, née Anne Gordon Colby, married Republican Rhode Island senator William Henry Vanderbilt III in 1929. Mrs. Vanderbilt participated in her husband's political career, helping him win his 1938 election as governor. While her husband served as a captain in the Naval Reserve during World War II, she helped to found the Ships Service Committee in New York City.

Clifton Webb was a dancer, singer, and actor who appeared in major supporting and leading roles on Broadway from 1913 to 1947. While most of his Broadway shows were musicals, he also starred in productions of *Blithe Spirit* (1941) and *Present Laughter* (1946), in parts that his friend Noël Coward (see **Coward**) had originally written with in mind. Webb's work in films earned him Academy Award nominations for Best Actor in a Supporting Role in *Laura* (1944) and *The Razor's Edge* (1946), and Best Actor in a Leading Role in *Sitting Pretty* (1949). Tall, slender, and elegant, he remained on Hollywood's best-dressed lists for decades.

Mrs. Sheldon Whitehouse, née Mary Crocker Alexander, was married to Sheldon Whitehouse, a career diplomat descended from a prominent New York family. She was the grandmother of U.S. Senator Sheldon Whitehouse, Democrat of Rhode Island.

Mrs. Wendell Wilkie, née Edith Wilk, was the wife of corporate lawyer and Republican presidential candidate Wendell Wilkie. A longtime Democrat, Wilkie switched political parties in 1939, after President Franklin D. Roosevelt's creation of the Tennessee Valley Authority put the nation's largest electric utility company, over which Wilkie presided, out of business. Wilkie then sought the Republican nomination, which he won after an unprecedented grassroots campaign. Although Roosevelt defeated him on election day, Wilkie campaigned against isolationism and racism in America, becoming in turn a Roosevelt ally.

About the Illustrators

Alajalov, a Russian-born painter, illustrator, and cartoonist whose work appeared in *The New Yorker*, the *Saturday Evening Post*, and *Vogue* provided all of the illustrations in this book (except that in the last chapter and those inserted by HarperCollins*Publishers* for this edition on pages 3, 21, 161, and 176). Alajalov also painted murals for the liner *America* and the Sherry Netherland Hotel in New York City.

Jean Pagès, a French-born Art Deco artist and illustrator who worked for *Vogue* and later designed New York restaurant La Caravelle's murals of Paris, created the illustration for the last chapter, "A New Bouquet of Recipes."

Clement Hurd, an American illustrator renowned for his collaborative work with Margaret Wise Brown on classic children's stories such as *Runaway Bunny* (1942) and *Goodnight Moon* (1947), illustrated and designed the original dust jacket.

Acknowledgments

To *mes petits chéris* Ben, Felix, and Leo, with many thanks to Bill Hall of High Valley Books, *un gentleman comme on n'en fait plus*, and to David Kuhn, *un agent hors pair*.

Index

———

Measurement
Conversion Chart
Imperial and Metric Equivalents

———

Liquid Measures

Fluid Ounces	U.S.	Imperial	Milliliters
—	1 teaspoon	1 teaspoon	5
¼	2 teaspoons	1 dessert spoon	7
½	1 tablespoon	1 tablespoon	15
1	2 tablespoons	2 tablespoons	28
2	¼ cup	4 tablespoons	56
4	½ cup or ¼ pint	—	110
5	—	¼ pint or 1 gill	140
6	¾ cup	—	170
8	1 cup or ½ pint	—	225
9	—	—	250, ¼ liter
10	1¼ cups	½ pint	280
12	1½ cups or ¾ pint	—	340
15	—	¾ pint	420
16	2 cups or 1 pint	—	450
18	2¼ cups	—	500, ½ liter
20	2½ cups	1 pint	560
24	3 cups or 1½ pints	—	675
25	—	1¼ pints	700
30	3¾ cups	1½ pints	840
32	4 cups	—	900
36	4½ cups	—	1000, 1 liter
40	5 cups	2 pints or 1 quart	1120
48	6 cups or 3 pints	—	1350
50	2½ pints	—	1400

Solid Measures

U.S. and Imperial Measures		Metric Measures	
Ounces	Pounds	Grams	Kilos
1	—	28	—
2	—	56	—
3½	—	100	—
4	¼	112	—
5	—	140	—
6	—	168	—
8	½	225	—
9	—	250	¼
12	¾	340	—
16	1	450	—
18	—	500	½
20	1¼	560	—
24	1½	675	—
27	—	750	¾
32	2	900	—
36	2¼	1000	1
40	2½	1100	—
48	3	1350	—
54	—	1500	1½
64	4	1800	—
72	4½	2000	2
80	5	2250	2¼
100	6	2800	2¾

Oven Temperature Equivalents

Fahrenheit	Celsius	Gas Mark	Description
225	110	¼	Cool
250	130	½	—
275	140	1	Very slow
300	150	2	—
325	170	3	Slow
350	180	4	Moderate
375	190	5	—
400	200	6	Moderately hot
425	220	7	Fairly hot
450	230	8	Hot
475	240	9	Very Hot
500	250	10	Extremely hot

The luxury of
uttering not one word

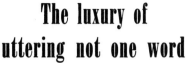

CLOSE by the head of every bed in the St. Regis Hotel, within easy reach of a lazily lifted hand, are two push buttons.

One calls the waiter to your door, the other calls the maid. Thus, when you wake in the morning, in that barely animate state between sleep and life, you do not need to fumble for the phone, or ask for "Room Service", or utter a single word to acquire a menu and order your breakfast.

True, that is perhaps a small thing for a sophisticated New York hotel to make a fuss about. But we're proud of it because it is symbolic of a number of small things we try to do to make life at the St. Regis a little more pleasant, a little more comfortable, a little more luxurious.

The bath towels are extra size; the face towels, sheets and pillow cases are of the finest Irish linen; the soap is a quality you would use at home; there's a tickless clock in every room. The prodigal size of these rooms would dismay an efficiency expert, and you could do an old-fashioned waltz in any of the bathrooms.

We endeavor to make St. Regis service a little different, too. It is not so much a regimented routine, as a philosophy of doing

thoughtful things in an unobtrusive way. No one presses you, no one forces service on you; but everyone does try to anticipate your wishes and carry them out graciously.

It would be presumptuous in this city of so many superb hotels to say any one is the finest. We have, as have our respected competitors, won many loyal friends amongst discerning people, and we'd like sometime to have the opportunity of bringing you into the St. Regis family.

THE St·Regis
FIFTH AVENUE AT 55TH STREET
NEW YORK

THE HOTEL THAT IS *NOT* "JUST LIKE HOME"